Owl

BRIEF COUNSELLING

BRIEF COUNSELLING

A practical guide
for beginning practitioners

WINDY DRYDEN and COLIN FELTHAM

Open University Press
Buckingham • Philadelphia

Open University Press
Celtic Court
22 Ballmoor
Buckingham
MK18 1XW

email: enquiries@openup.co.uk
world wide web: http://www.openup.co.uk

and
325 Chestnut Street
Philadelphia, PA 19106, USA

First Published 1992
Reprinted 1993, 1994, 1996 (twice), 1998, 1999

Copyright © Windy Dryden and Colin Feltham 1992

A catalogue record of this book is available from the
British Library

Library of Congress Cataloging-in-Publication Data

Dryden, Windy.
    Brief counselling: a practical guide for beginning practitioners
    Windy Dryden and Colin Feltham.
        p.   cm.
    Includes bibliographical references and index.
    ISBN 0–335–09972–6 (pbk.)
    1. Short-term counseling.   I. Feltham, Colin, 1950–   .
II. Title.
    [DNLM: 1. Counseling – methods.   WM 55 D799b]
BF637.C6D78   1992
158'.3–dc20
DNLM/DLC
for Library of Congress   92–8610
                                                            CIP

Typeset by Graphicraft Typesetters Limited, Hong Kong
Printed in Great Britain by St Edmundsbury Press Limited
Bury St Edmunds, Suffolk

For Marie

CONTENTS

Part III   Initiating change

Part IV   Encouraging change through homework

Contents

Part V Counselling in the middle phase

ACKNOWLEDGEMENTS

The authors would like to acknowledge the authors and pub-
lishers for kind permission to reproduce the following material as
appendices to the volume.
Appendix 1 Stages of change questionnaire, courtesy of J.
Prochaska.
Appendix 2 Opinions about psychological problems question-
naire (Part 1: Causes of psychological problems). Chris Barker,
Nancy Pistrang and David A. Shapiro, unpublished manuscript,
Department of Psychology, University College London, Gower
St., London WC1E 6BT.
Appendix 3 Opinions about psychological problems question-
naire (Part 2: Help for psychological problems). Chris Barker,
Nancy Pistrang and David A. Shapiro, unpublished manuscript,
Department of Psychology, University College London, Gower
St., London WC1E 6BT.
Appendix 4 Possible reasons for not completing homework as-
signments questionnaire. Professor Windy Dryden (1990) *Rational-
Emotive Counselling in Action*. London: Sage.
Appendix 7 Specimen 'goodbye letters'. Dr A. Ryle (1990)
Cognitive-Analytic Theory: Active Participation in Change.
Chichester: Wiley, pp. 43 and 47. Reprinted by permission of
John Wiley & Sons Ltd.
Appendix 8 Case evaluation form. Professor S.L. Garfield (1989)
The Practice of Brief Psychotherapy. Oxford: Pergamon, p. 132.
    The authors would also like to thank Pat Bizley for the statistical
information on uptake of counselling at Leicester Polytechnic
Counselling and Welfare Service.

INTRODUCTION

Purpose and structure of the book

As the title states, this is a book of practical advice. It is designed to help you examine and improve your work with clients in brief counselling. It is not intended as a definitive manual, as a theoretical tract, or as a new model of counselling. (For a comprehensive treatment of brief psychotherapy, see Wells and Gianetti 1990.) We are interested in offering guidelines from a broad perspective. The ideas in this book are culled from our own experiences as seasoned practitioners of brief counselling as well as from our work as supervisors and trainers of counsellors. From the latter, we know that the kinds of questions raised here are frequently asked by trainee and beginning counsellors. Our aim is to raise these questions as issues to be discussed on training courses and in supervision. It is not our intention to convey a series of injunctions; rather, we wish to sensitise you to important issues in brief counselling. What you will find here is not what you *should* do, but what you might wish to consider in your work with clients. We have in some cases cited our own views and our own work with clients, but these are best regarded as *our* views, as illustrations and discussion points.

This book gives a process view of brief counselling. Where we have given examples of work with clients, this is in order to illustrate various points of the counselling process. We have laid the book out in six parts for practical reasons, but not to suggest that the counselling process necessarily follows such a structure. Also, we have presented a list of items in broad sequence, but we fully realise that in practice counselling does not easily fit into a neat ordered sequence. We suggest, then, that you use the book in a way that suits you, your point of development as a counsellor, and the issues facing you in your work with each of your clients. You may become aware that certain issues are relevant to different clients at different times. One of our hopes is that you will discuss these issues with your fellow trainees, other counsellors, and your supervisor.

The emphasis in this book is a practical one. We have reproduced some questionnaires as appendices and you may wish to use or adapt these for your own purposes. We realise that certain approaches to counselling do not readily lend themselves to particular interventions. The use of homework assignments, for example, is a topic which may arouse some dissent in certain quarters. We have not assumed that any particular counselling orientation is more fitting for brief counselling than any other, but of course we do bring our own views and orientations to this book. We have given various examples in the book of how practitioners from different schools might regard particular issues. We do suggest that you consider what role assessment, goalsetting, homework and other issues might play in helping each of your clients effectively in a relatively short time. We recognise, too, that certain of the items listed will not apply at all to some clients. Use this practical advice flexibly in the service of your clients.

What is brief counselling?

We follow the view that there is no essential distinction between counselling and psychotherapy. Both activities aim to alleviate human suffering, solve problems and help people live more satisfying lives. We disagree with commentators who define counselling as a superficial, brief, symptom-removing activity which compares unfavourably with the 'real' work of (long-term and 'in-depth') psychotherapy. One psychotherapist, for example (Storr 1963: 2), suggested that 'psychotherapy which involves more than superficial guidance is bound to be of some length, often of very considerable length'. Length of treatment has been a contentious issue since the time of Freud, and the debate continues to this day, not only within the psychoanalytic camp but also from a humanistic perspective. John Rowan, for example, in his interview with Windy Dryden (1992) regards brief therapy as threatening to cheat clients of an opportunity to explore their lives in depth. It is psychoanalytic practitioners who have, in fact, been in the forefront of efforts to condense therapy (see Flegenheimer

1982) and these efforts have been helped by the emergence of behavioural and cognitive-behavioural methods, as well as, latterly, by integrative models like cognitive-analytic therapy (Ryle 1990). For more detailed comparisons of brief and long-term models of therapy, see Budman and Gurman (1988: 11) and Malan (1975: 8). Please note that we are not claiming superiority for brief counselling and we address the subject of necessary referrals to long-term work within this book.

Brief counselling refers to any counselling that lasts from one session to approximately twenty sessions. Malan (1975) cites cases of brief psychotherapy ranging from four to fifty sessions. The exact number of sessions to be cited as evidence of counselling being brief is not our concern here, and we shall assume that you, our readers, will be dealing with many clients who see you for anything from a few to twenty or so sessions. We also need to point out that there are various patterns of counselling contract. Twenty sessions, for example, may either be consecutive weekly sessions, or spread over a year. Rosenbaum et al. (1990) present the 'challenge of single-session therapies' which recognise 'decisive moments of life' and call for the intensive use of therapeutic skills. Many commercial, statutory and voluntary agencies offer a maximum of six or eight sessions. Mann (1973) pioneered time-limited psychotherapy consisting of twelve sessions, the non-negotiability of which reflected, in his view, the reality of life and death, and imperfection. Ryle's (1990) model offers sixteen sessions, partly for economic reasons but also partly in order to maximise commitment and minimise unhealthy dependency. Budman and Gurman (1988) advocate a model of brief therapy which is phased out by the tapering-down of sessions; but they also conceive of therapy as a recurring process, to be used as a kind of 'mental health check-up' with reference to developmental crises. A technical distinction between brief counselling and time-limited counselling is that the former does not specify a limited number of sessions or an ending date, even though it may last only for weeks or months.

Why brief counselling?

Long-term therapy or counselling is not widely available through the National Health Service in the UK (or elsewhere), nor do private health insurance companies recognise its necessity. Private long-term therapy, particularly of the pure psychoanalytic variety (four or five times a week for several years) is very expensive and totally inaccessible to most people. As Albee (1990) has pointed out, psychotherapy is so labour-intensive, so time-consuming and costly, that its impact on the mental health of the population as a whole is infinitesimal. Add to this the first-hand reports of some former consumers of psychotherapy (see, for example, some of the accounts in Dinnage 1988) and their claims of wasted years in analysis, and you will agree, perhaps, that the length and cost of therapy requires serious investigation. As Fairbairn and Fairbairn (1987: 22) put it:

> the way in which professional time, expertise and energy is used is one of the primary issues in resource allocation in all of the caring professions: indeed the justification of the way in which human effort is utilised is common to those who adopt a thoughtful stance in all of human enterprise.

Analysts like Malan (1975) and Balint et al. (1972) took up the challenge to reduce the length of therapy. They seemed to agree that 'focal' concerns helped to shorten therapy, and that attention to the use of time and judicious exclusion of certain kinds of client material were important factors in achieving change more efficiently. Focal concerns, as defined by Balint et al. (as well as other writers) combine identified limited aims in counselling and identified conflicts in the client's life. The gradual emergence of behavioural and humanistic models of therapy stimulated research into therapeutic outcome and process and encouraged practitioners to experiment with other models and to integrate them into their own work. Many new schools of therapy appeared in recent decades (including Gestalt therapy, primal therapy and transactional analysis), each often claiming to be briefer than previous models. As Malan (1975) has suggested, there does seem to be a phenomenon of 'waning enthusiasm' on the part of therapists (who cannot summon the intense energy and interest they once had) which is perhaps responsible for promisingly brief therapies growing inevitably longer. Against this background of innovation and research, a combination of economic restraints and the growing popularity of counselling has led to an awareness that non-medical counsellors can help to effect personal change in relatively brief periods of counselling.

Budman (1990: 209) writes that 'of all the individuals who visited mental health outpatient settings in this country [USA] in 1980, nearly 70 per cent came for six or fewer visits'. Garfield (Garfield and Bergin 1986: 217) demonstrated that various surveys revealed that clients frequently terminated therapy after six, eight or ten sessions. This is what Budman and Gurman (1988) refer to as 'brief therapy by default', since clients terminated without notice. Increasingly, it seems to be emerging that clients who drop out of counselling 'early' may well have got all the help they perceive themselves as needing for the time being, within the first few sessions. Many student counselling services report that they see clients on average for only two, three or five sessions, by the client's choice; the service is free and there is no limit set to how many sessions are available to students. (For the year 1990/91, for example, Leicester Polytechnic Counselling and Welfare Service saw 490 clients from a total student population of 11,922, who attended an average of four sessions (74 per cent of clients attended for only one session): University College London Student Counselling Service in that same period saw 250 clients from a total student population of 9,138, for an average of four to five sessions.)

There is also some evidence that brief therapy is as effective as long-term therapy (Shlien et al. 1962). Taken together, such research indications suggest that the reality is that most counselling and therapy is in fact brief; that clients wish it to be brief; and that its brevity does not detract from its effectiveness. For these reasons, many contemporary counsellors, including ourselves, advocate brief counselling 'by design'. Unfortunately, many training courses still fail to address this reality.

Who is brief counselling for?

We recognise that there are people for whom brief therapy or counselling is not appropriate. We address this subject explicitly within the text. In general, it is not suitable for people with chronic disturbances including drug and alcohol addictions, personality disorders and serious mental health problems – although Ryle (1990) claims that cognitive-analytic therapy has been successful with people diagnosed as having personality disorders. Perry (1989), however, advocates 'intermittent continuous therapy' for clients with 'borderline' and 'personality disorder' diagnoses. Many time-limited therapists advocate strict selection procedures to ensure optimal prognoses for treatment. We believe that you can afford to be less selective than many of these practitioners. Interestingly, Holmes and Lindley (1989) suggest that brief therapy, although more appealing to working-class clients because of its goal-directedness, is also less likely to be offered because working-class clients are commonly seen (so Holmes and Lindley claim) as being less articulate and as exhibiting their disturbances in more of the addictive and suicidal categories of behaviour (and are therefore more likely to be prescribed medication).

We believe that candidates for brief counselling should not be severely disturbed. They should preferably be in the 'neurotic range' of life crises, mild anxieties and depressions; they are likely to be people experiencing what Budman and Gurman (1989) refer to as 'interpersonal-developmental-existential' (IDE) problems or concerns. This implies that clients' problems are not necessarily rooted in their pasts. Your brief counselling clients should preferably be functioning reasonably well and be able to benefit from a therapeutic process that will last months rather than years. They should be capable of formulating their problems reasonably succinctly. Thus, applicants for counselling who are either seriously psychiatrically disturbed or preoccupied with metaphysical questions about the meaning of life may need to be referred to alternative appropriate services. Brief counselling lends itself best to what Nelson-Jones (1989) calls 'pragmatic existentialism', which suggests a concern of client and counsellor alike for dealing with matters in a finite, problem-solving manner.

'Who or what is best for this individual?'

The above question is put by Lazarus and Fay (1990). We wish to underscore the importance of this question. On no account try to fit your clients to what is in this (or any other) book: pick from the book what meets your clients' needs. As an example of flexibility, Budman and Gurman (1988) are willing to include significant people in clients' lives in therapy sessions in order to facilitate needed change. However, unless you have had training in couple or family work, we do not recommend that you do this, even though it can be helpful.

So use this book as a reference for raising issues. Note anything that provokes something relevant to your clients. Take to your supervisor any issues about which you are uneasy, unsure or excited. You will note that we advocate throughout the book that you invite your client's feedback on the counselling process. This will enable you to fine-tune your work. It may also arise that you are not the best person for your client. We wish to make this point clearly: since the success of counselling rests at least in part on the relationship between client and counsellor, and since you are often in a more powerful position than your client, do consider whether you are the best resource for the client.

We have made this last point in various ways throughout the book and it is not intended to be demoralising. It applies to experienced and inexperienced counsellors alike. Perhaps this is a good point at which to state, too, that the success of brief counselling depends not only on the therapeutic relationship, but also on your understanding and using skilfully a range of techniques (see Hill 1989). We hope that this book will be an aid to you in developing your skills further. Finally, we want to make the point that one of your best assets as a beginning counsellor is your level of enthusiasm. Durlak (1979), reviewing research on the effectiveness of paraprofessionals (e.g. students and volunteers) and professionals, concluded that paraprofessionals were perceived as at least as effective as professional helpers, and in some cases more so. Although some commentators have queried these results, our view is that if they hold true it is likely that the degree of enthusiasm of paraprofessionals is a beneficial factor for work with clients. So an overarching guideline might be: retain your enthusiasm, be open to new ideas, but temper this with a healthy scepticism! We wish you well in your work. Finally, if you are aware of areas of concern for which you would like to see practical guidance provided in any future editions of this book, we would welcome your comments. If so, please send any ideas to us, care of the publisher.

PART I

Orienting the client to counselling

Understanding the educational
system

1 Recognise that the client reacts to you from the first contact

When is the first contact with a client made? Although some people regard the first meeting in person as the first working contact, we take the view that the first contact is usually, and significantly, that made by telephone or letter. Let's deal with the telephone first. Assuming that you're not exclusively a telephone counsellor, this is the way in which most of your clients do their initial reaching out for help. It's a big step for most people. Most are 'first-time buyers'; they may be very distressed, unsure of what they want (and need) and nervously unfamiliar with counselling. They don't know you and may have only the barest of information about you. Alternatively, but less likely, they may be informed consumers, ready to question how you work. What is going on in this apparently short and simple phone call, and how might you, as the counsellor, best be prepared for it? Brandt (1982) contends that counsellors are quite likely to be involved in various activities and thoughts when the phone rings, which will colour the way they respond to a new client's call. Brandt believes that this is the point at which slightly distorted mutual impressions begin to form and subsequently to affect the relationship.

Our preference, and recommendation, is not to become involved in counselling at this stage. Don't invite lengthy explanations of the (potential) client's problems. However, do be courteous and welcoming. The person on the other end of the phone may become your client, and therefore this stage will form the beginning of the therapeutic alliance between you. (Even if they don't become your client, you may be able to help in a simple humanitarian way by offering information. Also, in some way you are an ambassador for the profession of counselling, and the way in which you respond may well influence the person's view of helping and helpers.)

Be prepared with what you will say about your availability, your fees, if you charge any, and your way of working. If the person doesn't ask about fees, for example, it is a good idea to give them the opportunity to do so by saying, 'Would you like to know how much my fees are?' This makes it easy for the less assertive client to ask and it clarifies for them whether or not they can afford your fee. If this is more than they can pay (and you do not operate a sliding scale) it is advisable that you have some idea of where they can look for a counsellor or counselling service that is within their price range. If they don't ask about your way of working, you might want to elicit enough information to determine whether you might be the right kind of counsellor for them or not. There can be misunderstandings about who you are, what counselling is, and so on, and this may be apparent at this stage. If it is, identifying it will save time and confusion.

If you have a telephone answering machine, record a message that is clear and welcoming and not an off-putting one. Any client who is tentative might easily be put off by a message verging towards the cold, clinical and businesslike. When you do receive messages from people enquiring about counselling, be sure to respond with as little delay as possible. The moment when people decide they really want to do something about a problem is a significant moment and holds a great potential for change. Again, when responding be as courteous and helpful as you can. As far as urgency goes, try to offer an appointment quickly, a place on a waiting list if appropriate, or a referral to another counsellor if timing is crucial and you cannot see the client yourself. Everything that has been said about telephone contact applies to letters except, of course, information conveyed by tone of voice and dialogue. But if you do receive letters asking for counselling or for information about your service, reply promptly, clearly and fully. If you have any literature that explains what you or your agency do, this can help the client to make a more informed decision.

If you work from an office or in an organisation, your potential clients may well speak first to a receptionist before speaking with you. Depending on the setting, the individual receptionist and his or her understanding of counselling, the client can get a variety of messages about the kind of counsellor you are and the kind of counselling experience that may be in store for them. As far as possible the receptionist should elicit the same kind of information and convey the same sort of welcome and sensitivity as you would want to. If you have any influence over this procedure, try to ensure that receptionists put across clear, warm messages and minimise any misunderstandings. In an agency where there is a team of counsellors, it is appropriate to ask applicants for counselling if they would prefer to see a man or woman, someone from a particular ethnic background (if available) and so on. You may want to ask whether they have any special access needs and give clear instructions about appointments (including the request that you be informed of any inability to attend or decision not to attend, in advance).

Ensure that clients know where to find you, where to wait, and whatever they need to know to feel reasonably comfortable. If you work in a particular way, for example with Gestalt, it is a good idea to explain, at least in the first session, the presence of large floor cushions or any other 'props', and in general to put clients at their ease (see Rowan 1988: Sklar 1988). On first meeting the client it is again, of course, extremely important that your welcome is as natural and courteous as possible. While some therapists, for therapeutic reasons, refrain from shaking hands or making eye contact or engaging in any 'chit-chat', we advocate an initially reassuring, warm welcome. Some clients may prefer some emotional distance, and some may prefer not to engage in any opening conversation, but we believe that most (certainly first-timers) will be helped more by a friendly welcome and naturalistic lead-in to counselling. You may want to consider what your building, consulting room, furnishings, and so on, convey to clients in terms of comfort, stimulation, fantasy or neutrality. For an interesting description of one therapist's view of 'the first five minutes' of a meeting with a new client, see Hobson (1985).

* Summary: Be prepared for telephone enquiries about counselling: be courteous and helpful, but avoid beginning counselling at this stage. Ensure that answering machines or intermediary staff are welcoming. Consider the messages conveyed by the setting in which you counsel.

2 Consider and introduce the subject of tape-recording

We place the subject of tape-recording here because you need to discuss it with your clients at the outset. You may or may not be familiar or comfortable with tape-recording your counselling sessions. It is a growing trend in counselling and a great deal has been learned by counsellors and researchers from listening to audiotapes. We are aware that many people are, however, unhappy with the practice, claiming that it upsets clients, inhibits spontaneity, threatens confidentiality, and so on. Also, some counsellors say that their clients are unwilling to be tape-recorded.

Let's look at this closely. First, let's consider the value, if not the indispensability, of taping. You can learn a lot from listening back over the session, with an ear to your manner, timing, intentions, clarity in responding and overall effectiveness. You can learn by comparing earlier with later sessions. You can even, if you wish, give copies of tapes to your clients for them to learn from. Even more important is the use of tapes in supervision. Without tapes, all your supervisor (or supervision group) hears, however astute she is, (or they are) is your inevitably selective account of your counselling. (We are not, however, advocating that you dispense with case discussion.) Research suggests, too, that even process recordings written soon after a counselling session exhibit selective memory and are a poor second best to audiotapes. Most people who do work with tape-recording attest to its benefits.

Second, let's look at how the issue of tape-recording is presented to your client. If you are convinced that taping will be beneficial and ethically sound, you are unlikely to encounter resistance to it from your client. Frequently, counsellors who are wary of using tapes convey their unease to the client and receive, in return, ambivalence or refusal from them. So our advice to you is to consider your own attitude carefully! Once convinced and ready to go, what will you say to your client? Be as honest and clear as you can. 'All counsellors are required to be supervised. I have found that one of the best ways of having work supervised is by listening to tape-recordings of actual sessions. The focus in supervision is on how I work, rather than on you. Naturally, everything heard or discussed is confidential and remains between the supervisor, who is a professional colleague, and myself.' Try some variant of that, to suit your own style. Perhaps the trickiest bit comes after this. Do you say. 'Is this OK with you?' or 'How do you feel about that?' (A closed versus an open question.) You need to consider how important taping is for monitoring the quality of your work and therefore how firm or negotiable you will be. After all, most counsellors are firm about time boundaries and fees, so where do you draw the line? Note, however, that if a client is genuinely reluctant or reticent about tape-recording it is better not to press the point.

You may work in an agency with a 'no taping' policy. Such a policy may be well-founded, or simply a tradition. Where it is the latter, we suggest you present the benefits of taping and negotiate for the right to do it. You may want to mention that one of the pioneers of such recordings was Carl Rogers.

Another issue you need to address is how long you will keep each tape, how you will arrange to keep it secure, and when you will erase or destroy it. Some counsellors tell their clients that tapes will be erased after they've been listened to, or after a period of six months or so. Some counsellors offer to give the tapes to the client. If you do this you may well need to stress that confidentiality applies both ways. Decide what to do on the basis of your own developmental needs and your ethical sensitivity. Some things cannot be left to chance, and protection of tapes, particularly where, for example, you may send them through the post to a supervisor, is one of these. (For reasons of geographical remoteness or where a counsellor practises a specialised form of therapy, and therefore has a specialist supervisor, supervision by post is sometimes practised.) Ensure that you have safeguards for any such transactions.

On the practical front, be sure to use a good quality recorder and external microphone, that batteries work and everything is switched on! There is nothing so frustrating as finding that a dynamic, learning-filled session has yielded a blank, fuzzy or inaudible tape. Try rehearsing the whole thing before actually doing it. Having said all this, we assure you that once you get into the habit of recording your work in this way, it will become as normal and non-intrusive as opening the door for your clients, invoicing them, or helping them to monitor their daily anxieties!

* **Summary: Consider the value of tape-recording your work, and any reservations you may have about it. Tapes offer you a wealth of material for supervision. Explain their use to clients: reassure clients about confidentiality: seek clients' permission to record. Check the practicalities of taping.**

---

3   Discover why the client is seeking counselling *now*

Counsellors are trained not to ask 'why' questions, of course, but one such question that inevitably arises when the client presents for counselling is 'Why now?'. Budman and Gurman (1988) make this a central consideration in their brief therapy model, and it is evident in many other approaches. But why ask it? We believe that the client's choice of when to seek counselling probably indicates something important: and that if you can understand why he has chosen this particular time, you may be in a good position to understand and exploit his motivation.

Budman and Gurman believe that timing is highly significant. They present an I-D-E schema, which stands for interpersonal, developmental and existential issues. What is happening in the person's life right now, in his relationships? How old is the client? Has he just had a birthday (for example, turned 40 and wondering where his life has gone)? Is it an anniversary of someone's death? What propels him to think about the meaning of his life now? What accidents may there have been in his life recently? People do not simply find themselves in counselling by chance. Often there is a crisis, precipitating a sudden inability to cope or a sudden need to reflect on life events. Sometimes it seems as if there is no obvious crisis at all. When asked what's brought them to counselling some clients claim they 'just don't know'. But later they may refer to a divorce, death or other crisis. So don't take your clients' 'I don't know' at face value – listen carefully for the precipitating factors.

As Budman and Gurman point out, many clients claim that they've 'always' been this way (depressed, lethargic, aimless). Sometimes a little probing and focusing reveals, however, that they have enjoyed quite different moods and experiences at other times, and that the present state can be identified as specific in time. Having in mind the question 'Why now?' helps you to press for such specifics. Often people cope fairly well with adversity until 'the straw that breaks the camel's back' arrives on the scene. When you maintain a focal perspective (identifying and working on the client's specific concerns), you are looking for the straws. What is it that makes this client think she can't cope? This isn't to say that everything was fine before the crisis, but that there is a crisis, and by identifying it you may have access to a mine of useful information.

Part of the 'why now?' is the client's declaration of discomfort, pain and need for change. What has happened? Have family dynamics changed? Is money a problem? Is the client no longer able to pretend to himself that he's going to become a concert pianist or run a marathon? There is a richness in the timing of seeking counselling, but its reasons are not always obvious. Some people put up with terrible suffering for a long time. Colin knew a woman who was sexually abused for years as a girl, which led to self-mutilation, shoplifting, alcohol and drug abuse. But she finally started to tell her story: she could bear it no longer. Exactly why this was the time that she chose, it's hard to say, but if she had been regarded as 'just another shoplifter' or 'just another addict' the emergence of her terrible story might have been delayed. Martin Buber (1947) tells the story of how he once had a casual conversation with a man who soon afterwards killed himself. This shocked Buber into realising that when people sought him out for 'casual' conversations, their motives and timing were usually far from casual.

One way to look at this question is 'Why not before?'. If your client's story is true, that everything has always been awful, then why has she not sought counselling earlier? It may be because she had become habituated to the bleakness of her life, but even so, why should she bother to try to change it? Amato and Bradshaw's (1985) study of delayed helpseeking lists reasons for delay which range from the client thinking he could solve it himself to lack of money.

You may also come across the client who has had counselling before (once, twice, or countless times). In this case, to ask the question 'Why now?' carries a different meaning. 'If you have had counselling often and over a long time span, then what might counselling do for you now that it hasn't done before?' would be a good question to ask, or to bear in mind. Exactly how you put these questions depends on your style and on the context. It is not always wrong to ask 'Why?' but there are ways of investigating that do not make the client feel fired at. 'I'm really interested to know what got you to come for counselling at this point in your life' conveys warm interest, for example. By taking seriously your clients' present predicament and present needs, you are respecting their frame of reference and using the time economically.

* Summary: Consider, and find ways of asking, why your clients have come for counselling at this particular time in their life. What is the significance of it? What does it tell you about their motivation and about the best way to help them?

4 Find out what the referral agent said

By a referral agent we mean anyone who has been involved in advising the client to see you or who has actually made initial contact with you in person, by telephone or letter. Often this will be a doctor, psychiatrist or other medical or helping professional, but equally it may be a friend of the client, a family member, a boss or colleague. One reason you will want to know what the referral agent said to the client is to be clear about what preconceptions the client is bringing to counselling. These may be accurate and helpful, but they may be inaccurate and could get the counselling process off to a bad start if they are unknown.

To give some examples. The client may have been told that you work with particular problems (e.g. sexual dysfunctions) and you may not. The client may have wrong information about who you are. (Windy has been telephoned by women who thought he was Wendy, for example, and who needed to be asked, on discovering the error, if they were willing to see a man or not!) A friend of the client may have recommended that she sees you because he saw you and benefited enormously. However, that does not necessarily mean that you are the best person for your ex-client's friend. Sometimes people are given the wrong information completely – for example, that they will be attending group therapy – and may arrive in high anxiety. Let's now look at the kinds of expectations clients may arrive with, based on what they've been told.

What did the referral agent say about why they thought the client needed counselling? Some clients may arrive with the idea that there is something dreadfully wrong with them, based on someone else's exaggerated view. Some clients come to counselling only because they've been told they ought to, and this is not the best way to begin. In this case you will need to elicit whether, in spite of this, the client wants to make a genuine commitment of their own. A referring agent may have told the client exactly what they need from counselling (e.g. 'to boost your self-esteem' or 'to learn to relax'). The client, if compliant, may try to go along with this. You, as the counsellor, are at risk of mistaking the referral agent's views for your client's views if you don't elicit the client's own agenda. It is worth saying here that some referral agents, particularly established helping professionals, may prescribe the treatment your client is to get on your behalf. You may not agree with their assessment; you may not want to be pre-empted and you may not even be equipped to offer certain interventions. Sometimes, therefore, you may need to address, in a tactful or an assertive manner, these issues with other concerned professionals. But the most important question here is why the client has come. In her own mind, why is she here?

What did the referral agent say about counselling? We shall go into this in greater depth later, but here we are asking what ideas the referral agent has implanted. Are they accurate or not? Are they biased? Are they exaggerated? Are they over-prescriptive? In other words, what expectations has the client brought to counselling that have been engendered by someone else? It can be a very useful way of opening up a discussion to ask this question and to lead into what the client thinks counselling is or can be. It is then also an opportunity for you to correct any misperceptions.

What did the referral agent say about you, the counsellor? Have you been presented as a medical expert, a friendly soul, a cheap psychotherapist, an advice-giver, or as someone who never gives advice? Discussing these points allows misunderstandings and fantasies to be aired and, hopefully, allows the client to engage more directly with you, thus establishing the beginnings of therapeutic work. You may need to correct erroneous ideas about who you are and what you can offer. (This might also apply, by the way, to written information about you or about counselling methods that the client has read and that may be inaccurate, partial or out of date.)

Your client may have been told by a friend, say, that she has a serious problem in relating to men. She may have been shocked and impressed and started to have all sorts of fantasies about the meaning of this. Her friend may exert a lot of influence over her. She may come into counselling with this agenda. Now, her friend may have accurately pin-pointed a problem, but it may not be the problem that the client is primarily concerned with, or it may be just one of many ways in which an underlying problem manifests itself. It can help to ask the client how she reacted to her friend's assessment of her concerns. Does she agree? What did the friend mean by it? Can she recall how she reacted at the time? And what has she made of it since? Has she been brooding on it? What thoughts lead from it? Getting back to the point at which she began considering coming for counselling is a valuable exercise because it enables the client's various motivations to be teased out. It is an important shift for people to make between entertaining the vague idea of counselling and actually seeking it. Another vital point is that people often feel motivated to consider making changes, yet realise that this feels threatening to them (see Section 8 regarding client fears). So to examine how they felt on first entertaining the idea of seeking counselling and how they feel now can be enormously important.

* **Summary: Ask clients who has encouraged them to come for counselling, and what advice or impressions they have been given. Allow any misconceptions and inaccurate information to be aired and corrected if necessary.**

---

5   Assess whether brief counselling is the most appropriate form of help

---

As we have noted in our introduction, most counselling in fact turns out to be relatively brief. You will eventually make your own decisions about how you prefer to work and you may come to discourage very short counselling contracts. Or you may do mostly long-term work, interspersed with briefer contracts. However, when confronted with a new client you need to assess in some way whether brief counselling is appropriate or not. Does the client have obvious focused concerns, or does the client have broad issues which can readily be broken down into specific areas of concern? Where clients have a broad 'personal growth' agenda, this can be addressed by brief counselling provided that they are willing and able to focus on specific concerns or aspirations within that agenda.

How do you help your client to focus in this way? When a client says, 'I don't know. I just feel generally unfulfilled', you need to be able to help her to make this concrete. Asking 'Can you tell me one or two of the ways in which you feel unfulfilled?' or 'I'd like you to tell me about a recent, specific example of this feeling' helps to make things workable. At this early stage of counselling, however, we are looking at how you assess the appropriateness of brief work. In this example, if it seemed clear that your client could not answer in a focused way, then another form of help may be indicated. You may decide to work in a longer-term, more exploratory way with her, or to refer her on.

A good indicator of whether a client will benefit from this kind of brief model is the nature of his pre-therapy relations. Has he had some good relationships with significant others? Has he spent a lot of time living alone? Has he had a very disrupted history (e.g. being taken into care as a child, being hospitalised, divorced, isolated)? Let us make it clear that these considerations are not intended as labelling exercises. What we want to get across is that the client's history of relating to other people is probably going to indicate the level of difficulty he will have in relating to you. If he has had good relationships, then he has an internalised experience of a joint alliance, and what he needs to have with you is just such a working alliance. So the chances are that if he says he is unable to get on with people, lives alone and rarely socialises, then you will have some difficulty in establishing a good working relationship within the limits of brief counselling. At the very least, you can expect that such a case will be a long-term prospect, and it may contain a lot of challenges. You have to decide whether you want to offer the time and whether you have the expertise. Strupp (1980) presents an interesting comparative study of such cases and their outcomes.

A further, and crucial, indicator of how successful brief counselling may be is the stage of change clients are at. Here we refer to the work of Prochaska and DiClemente (1984), which sets out the pre-contemplative, contemplative, action, maintenance and relapse model of stages of change (see Section 18). For our purposes here, pre-contemplation refers to that phase in which people do not consider they have a problem, or may dimly and distantly feel some discomfort but have no specific idea or intention regarding making changes. Contemplation is the phase in which a problem or problems are in conscious awareness. Not only do people realise that there is something uncomfortable and pressing but they are considering doing something about it. This is of course the stage in which people frequently enter counselling. It is important to note that this may be a tentative time. People may slip back into the pre-contemplative stage. They may certainly take their time to be fully committed to change. But evidence of a contemplative level of motivation is crucial when considering whether a client will benefit from brief counselling. You could well be wasting your client's and your own time if you try to persist with counselling when he is clearly not ready.

In looking at these issues you will be getting some idea of your client's level of motivation. Is he here because he wants to be? Is this time in his life significant enough to push him into counselling? And does he have an understanding that he must be an active partner in the process, rather than a passive consumer? Can you see evidence that he will be able to stay the course? If the answer is a predominant 'yes', then you can feel reasonably confident in moving ahead with brief counselling. If the answers are negative, then you may need to take more time to help the client towards readiness and commitment, or alternatively consider referral to other resources.

Tied in with the ability to specify what their current problems are is what clients' future goals are. Elicit at this stage how your client envisages change. Unless there is some idea of where she wants to aim, there is a risk that the counselling process may get bogged down in interesting but not progressive work. Having goals (which can, of course, be modified) helps to serve as a bridge between past and future, between problems and solutions, and between counselling and self-realisation. Unfortunately, some counsellors and clients forget at times that counselling itself is not the goal, but that change and autonomy for the client in her everyday life is what counselling is for. Does your client have goals, and can she realistically head towards, modify and attain her goals? Remind yourself (later in the process) of why the client entered counselling in the first place, if you are tempted to protract counselling or if you and your client run into impasses.

Lastly, as an indicator of the appropriateness of brief counselling, consider the everyday networks in which the client lives. Does she have a good supportive environment? Are there friends or family who will support her efforts at change and be available in times of difficulty? And conversely, are there significant others in her life who may be destructive, eroding what the counselling may be building, undermining the new energy and strength she is gaining? In discussing this, both you and the client will be able to assess and anticipate any potential set-backs. If she has little support, or has friends who are antagonistic to her coming for counselling, she will face more obstacles. Has she the strength to deal with these? Is there some way she can find other resources for support? How can you best help her through such obstacles? Such discussions will help cement an understanding of brief counselling and its appropriateness for the client.

* **Summary: Consider whether brief focal counselling is something you are happy to practise. Discover whether your clients have well-defined concerns and goals. Consider what stage of change they are at – whether they have had good enough**

relationships previously (as a sign that they can relate to you) –
and what social supports they have.

---

6   Refer if appropriate

If necessary, we commend the practice of referring a client on,
either at the telephone stage or soon thereafter. There is a danger
that some counsellors can come to think of themselves as God's
gift to clients, and therefore arrogantly dismiss the idea of referral; or have economic reasons for not referring clients on (you
need the business); or a rationale that your way of working pro-
hibits pre-judging clients and the seriousness of their difficulties
(and that you must therefore take on everyone for counselling).
Let's remember that clients are consumers who have a right to
the best possible service, and also that they are often distressed,
which means that the sooner they get the right help (rather than
hit-or-miss treatment) the better. You may well be the best choice
of counsellor for many or most of those people who come to you,
or you may be as good as many other counsellors (or you may not
be!). Your client may live in an area where there are no other
counsellors, in which case the idea of referral may be irrelevant.
But do give proper thought to your ability to provide each client
with what they need.

Do not succumb to the idea that you are a failure as a counsellor if you feel a need to refer. You may well not have the
experience to deal with particular clients and you will be acting
responsibly if you refer someone on if you are in doubt. Referring
on implies, of course, familiarity with other counsellors and their
work, and with other local services. We certainly advocate that
you familiarise yourself with colleagues locally (for example by
joining BAC – the British Association for Counselling – and other
organisations, and their local branches). Also, it is a good idea to
know something about local (or even national) agencies offering
specialised services. There are specialist agencies working in the
areas of mental health, marital distress, eating disorders, sexual
abuse, and many others. If you can't help someone, try to refer
them on, or at the very least direct them to the reference section
of the local library, or give them the phone number of BAC,
Relate, Cruse, or whatever is appropriate.

There may be various reasons for referring on. It may emerge that this person's problem would be better addressed through couple counselling or in group therapy or the client may want and benefit from long-term psychotherapy. It may become very clear that the client wants a particular kind of therapy. You may think of a colleague whose experience and/or orientation closely matches the needs of this client. You may get the feeling that a counsellor of the opposite sex, or someone older, or someone who can speak another language, may be more appropriate for the client than you are. For example, your client may have clear signs of an obsessive-compulsive disorder, and you realise that he'll be better off getting some medication and behaviour therapy than psychodynamic counselling from you. A woman client may tell you that she is being beaten by her husband, and you may suggest she seeks a refuge. Since some people perceive counselling as a kind of befriending, you may have to refer this kind of person on to a befriending scheme. Some people, let's say with agonising headaches, may be afraid of doctors and believe that counselling is what they need. You may have to encourage them gently to see a doctor (perhaps helping them to explore their fears, but not trying to substitute for medical attention). Or a client may not be able to afford your services for very long and you may not offer a free counselling service.

All of the above not only implies familiarity with other services but also implies a readiness to act in the interests of the client. It is unprofessional to ignore such issues. Besides that, however, we believe you will work more effectively and more happily if you learn to identify people with whom you work well, and learn which people are better referred on. Some counsellors no doubt worry that some clients will feel rejected if they are advised to go elsewhere. Look at it, rather, as being in the client's interests that she gets the best service. It may well be you, but if it isn't, don't hesitate to let her know. ('I appreciate how you feel about these problems', you might say, 'and I might be able to help somewhat, but I happen to know someone who has particular experience in this area, and I think you would find that she is best placed to help you.') Also remember that while you refer on to colleagues, they may well refer people on to you, and this is a persuasive reason for knowing your local colleagues and their way of working.

A more difficult area, perhaps, is when your client does indeed need counselling, and perhaps even the kind of counselling that you offer, but for some reason you realise that you are not going to get on. In theory all counsellors treat the first session as an opportunity to decide whether they can work together with new clients, but in practice it is probably rare that any counsellor or client would say. 'No, I don't like you', or 'I'm sorry, but you remind me too much of my mother' or even 'I can't relate to someone who is sexist, or who has an obvious public school background'. Sometimes such interpersonal obstacles can be explored and used to good effect in subsequent counselling. Since there are research findings suggesting that a good fit between client and counsellor is optimal for a good outcome, if you notice doubts on your part or your clients', relating to these sorts of issues, or even more subtle personality factors, raise them sensitively for discussion.

Obviously if you are just beginning to counsel it will often be hard to know if you are right for each client, and if you are inclined towards self-doubt you may want to refer every client on to a more experienced counsellor! This is not the message we want to give here. We simply suggest that you don't feel obliged to take on everyone, that you bear referral in mind, and that you prepare yourself by becoming acquainted with colleagues and other services.

* Summary: Don't automatically take on everyone for counselling who makes an enquiry. Consider the kind of help most appropriate for each client and whether you can offer it. Assess how good the fit is between you and the client. Familiarise yourself with other colleagues and services. Don't interpret the need to refer on as a failure on your part.

---

7 Consider and spell out the limits of confidentiality

We consider it essential that clients are made fully aware of the nature and limits of confidentiality at the outset of counselling. Some counsellors may not give much explanation of confidentiality or other practicalities and boundaries. We are in favour of explicit discussion of certain matters and confidentiality is one of the most important of these.

Confidentiality needs to be clear to you, the counsellor, from the very beginning. Suppose, for example, that before you've even seen your client for the first time, his mother telephones you and wants to talk about him. You must make it clear that you will not discuss her son with her, since he is your client and your work with him is confidential. Or suppose that you are seeing a husband and a wife separately, each for individual counselling. Your contract is with each one, and confidentiality should remain with each one. You may be given information by one about the other, which you may find taxing to 'put aside', but you are obliged not to share it. (It should be noted that some counsellors would not see both partners under such circumstances, but you must decide where you stand on this.)

Is it enough to say, 'Counselling is confidential'? We think not, since it says very little and is usually not entirely true. What is usually meant is that counselling is confidential within certain limits. These are as follows. Since all counsellors must be supervised, they must discuss their work with supervisors, and therefore clients will be discussed. Some people prefer to talk about their clients anonymously in supervision, or to refer to them by initials or some other disguise. This is up to you. What is important is to let your client know that this is the case. You may discuss them with your supervisor or supervision group, and your clients should know this. They should, however, be reassured that all discussion remains confidential at that level and is for the purpose of professional enhancement only. Related to supervision is the expectation of you as the counsellor, if you work in a particular setting, or sometimes submit written reports on a client. In this case, it is best to discuss it openly with the client and ask if there is anything they would prefer you not to include.

An instance in which confidentiality may be tested is where you as the counsellor have grounds for believing that your client is a danger to himself or others. Put this straightforwardly. Windy says to his clients. 'If in my judgement you became a risk to yourself or to others and you didn't realise it, I would need to confer with other professionals. Is this acceptable to you?' Nothing binds you to making this statement, but we recommend some variant of it in the interests of clarity and honesty. Some counsellors, in fact, attempt to guarantee total confidentiality, including immunity from this kind of instance. We advise you to consult BAC's Code of Ethics and Practice to satisfy yourself as to where the line is drawn. Consider your own position. How will you deal with it in those probably very rare instances when it occurs? For example, if your client admits to having recently sexually abused a child, it is appropriate to confront him and ask him either to take appropriate action himself, or to give you permission to do so on his behalf. But it is advisable to have forewarned him of the possibility of this latter eventuality.

Now, this may seem like a lot to get across without alarming your clients. We don't suggest you read them the Riot Act, as it were, either at the beginning of counselling or later. Rather, find your own way of putting it, and present it sensitively. If the client is in distress and needing to talk, you will not choose this moment to go over all this. But it is best to make it clear at a very early stage. You cannot assume that clients know exactly what confidentiality means and where it ends. It can be very containing to be told clearly what the ground rules are. It gives clients the opportunity to decide, if there is anything extremely delicate or bordering on violence or criminality, whether counselling is the right place for them to bring their problems.

* Summary: Introduce the subject of confidentiality at the very outset of counselling. Talk explicitly, clearly and honestly about the limits of confidentiality. Present the subject sensitively, but be prepared to confront the client and take appropriate action if necessary.

---

8   Explore the client's fears about counselling

In discussing confidentiality we have touched on one of the fears that clients may well have about counselling. But there are others. Several research studies have revealed a number of common such fears:

1   Is counselling what I need?
2   Will I be treated as a 'case'?
3   Will I be taken seriously?
4   Will the counsellor share my values?
5   Will the counsellor think me a bad person?
6   Will the counsellor think I'm more disturbed than I am?
7   Will the counsellor discover things I don't want him/her to?

   8 Will the counsellor be competent?
   9 Will I be pressurised into doing things I don't want to?
 10 Will my friends think I'm crazy?
 11 Will I find out things I don't want to know?
 12 Will I lose control of myself?
(These items are taken from Pipes et al. 1985.)

It is very evident that clients fantasise about what their counselling and counsellor will be like, what the setting will be like, and
how they (the clients) will handle, or fail to handle, their anxiety.
Anxieties are sometimes elicited by certain settings (e.g. psychiatric hospital) or by certain professionals and their status and
power. A common element throughout, however, is vulnerability.
The client is distressed or confused and is about to acknowledge
this to a stranger. He is hopeful of a solution and is putting
himself into a stranger's hands. He probably does not know the
ropes, although he will probably imagine various things about
counselling based on images received through the media or
stories heard from friends, or from books.

   It is clear from the list above that people do not want to feel
dehumanised or stigmatised. They feel that they are putting
themselves on the line, baring their emotions, and in order to do
that there is a need to feel some assurance that the counsellor is
competent and has integrity. Perhaps people sense that the counselling situation is one in which honesty and emotional freedom
is respected and even expected, but on first going into the situation
they cannot know what will come up, what surprises may emerge,
and how they will be affected. In this sense, then, it can look,
and feel, very frightening.

   You may remember from your own first experiences as a client
how frightening it can all be, but since you may work with raw
feelings and intimate stories day after day, you may inevitably
forget some of the strangeness and vulnerability involved for the
client. So, in being aware that people do bring these fears, and
often other, more personal, idiosyncratic fears, how will you deal
with them? Obviously time needs to be allowed for the expression of these fears, but will you just leave it to the client to come
out with it, or elicit anxieties by questioning? We are in favour
of putting it to clients that they may well feel a little unsure and
may have some question they want to ask of us. Anything that
gets across the idea that we are listening, interested, understanding and non-judgemental will be helpful for the client.
Sometimes a statement to the effect that counselling can be a

daunting experience, including reference to the kinds of common fears listed above, can relieve a client of the idea that he is the craziest and most undeserving person in the world. You need to find a way of putting this that does not ignore or minimise the possible enormity of his fears. Clients' recurrent questions about the normality of certain symptoms may indicate that there is a particular severity of problems. But remember that a certain level of anxiety often promotes movement in counselling. So we are not advocating a pacifying exercise but a sensitive attunement to the individual and readiness to explore his particular fears.

While these fears have been found to be commonly experienced among clients, identifying which ones your client has, and what, exactly, they mean to him, is likely to throw up rich material for your work together. It can form the basis for future work on irrational beliefs, for example. Or it can help to strengthen the trust between you, which can then be generalised into other everyday situations.

* Summary: Recognise that clients commonly enter counselling with fantasies and fears. Encourage them to air these and if necessary offer examples of common fears. Be alert to acute fears and anxieties. Use what is discussed to focus on concerns.

9   Find out the client's idea of how long counselling will last

Some clients are totally new to counselling and their ideas of how often they will be coming and for how long may well not accord with your own. In some cases people will expect counselling to compare with what they get from their general practitioner (GP), which is to say, perhaps, fifteen minutes today, with perhaps a follow-up two weeks later. Others may have seen television dramas showing people lying on couches day after day, and may expect to come and see you for some years. Some people certainly expect to see you for only one or two sessions. If you are working with the kind of brief model we are talking about here, then there could well be a mismatch between your idea and your client's. We would advise that this issue be aired and resolved.

You might ask, 'Have you thought about how long you might come for counselling?' This gives you the opportunity to hear some of the client's perceptions of counselling and perhaps to gauge how difficult they think their problems are. But it also allows for any misconceptions to surface and be resolved. For example, it may be that you will need to refer on, if the client wants to come three times a week for some years. Or you may decide that you will see them for a longer period after all. Or if they have in mind only a few visits, you might want to suggest that it would be fairer to them if they gave it more time. It can help to say that often a minimum of four or six sessions is advisable in order to assess matters or to let the counselling process begin to take effect, and that many people undertake counselling for a period of several months. (See section 78 in this book on different kinds of endings.) You might arrange a specific contract for a series of sessions followed by a review. Whatever you decide, it will unfold better by opening a discussion on expectations. It is also fair to the client when you give some picture of what may lay ahead in terms of time and financial commitment.

* **Summary: Help your clients to talk about their impressions of how long counselling will take. Look out for any discrepancy between the client's and your own views on length of counselling. Address any practical implications.**

---

10   Explore the client's past history of being helped

Many clients have had help with their problems before, some from counsellors and other professionals, and others from friends and family. We believe that there are good reasons for explicitly asking about clients' previous experiences of seeking and having help. Your client may have had a successful or unsuccessful experience. (Bad or 'neutral' experiences of help are sometimes called 'attempted solutions' or 'negative outcomes'.) Bearing in mind our suggestions about sensitively adjusting your questions to each client and the frame of mind they are in, we suggest you try to get the following kinds of information.

Find out whether your client has previously seen a counsellor, therapist or other helping professional. When was this? Under what circumstances? Ask these questions with interest, avoiding an interrogative style. As rapidly and skilfully as you can, you need to elicit the client's experience of whatever help she has had. The purpose of gathering this kind of information is to learn what to capitalise on and what to avoid. So ask the client what she found helpful and unhelpful about any previous counselling. Such a conversation might go something like this:

You: Have you had any counselling or similar help in the past?

Client: Well, I saw someone once or twice a few years ago, yes.

You: Can you tell me something about that experience, perhaps?

Client: Well, it was just that I was having a bad time then and I went to this 'drop-in' place and talked to a lady, a kind of psychologist, I think.

You: I see. I'd be interested to know how helpful that was for you – I mean, if you were having a bad time, in what way did this psychologist help?

Client: She listened to me. She was quite kind. She told me I should be more assertive.

You: And did that help?

Client: Yes and no, really. I mean, it helped in a way, to have someone interested in me, but it wasn't that easy for me. I mean, I couldn't just go out and be assertive.

You: And so, what happened? Did you stop seeing her?

Client: Yes. I meant to get in touch with her again, but I couldn't see how it would help.

What do we learn from this kind of dialogue? First, that our client has had a 'bad time' before, in life and perhaps in a helping situation too. (We can pursue this later.) Second, that she sought professional help and was offered some definite kind of help. At this stage we don't know if the 'psychologist' actually recommended that the client 'should' be more assertive or if this is what the client heard, but it still gives us some valuable information: it will be important not to come across as prescriptive. The client appreciates having interest shown in her. She is expressing a belief that assertiveness was or is difficult, but probably meaningful as an avenue for exploration. Evidently things did not work out, she was disillusioned and did not return. These pieces of data contain many warnings! However, they need not be read as facts and her feelings may have changed since that time. This kind of information is useful, but requires intelligent analysis and operationalising. Let's look at one way it might go:

Client: I just couldn't go out and be assertive.

You: That was too much for you at *that* time?

Client: Yes, I was very shy. I still am. Things have improved a bit, but recently, well, I just can't face some things.

You: So there have been some changes since then, but things are not as you'd like them at the moment. I wonder – is there anything the psychologist could have done that might have helped you more in the long run?

Client: Mmm. Well, I suppose if I hadn't felt so rushed. Maybe if there had been longer to talk, to unwind ...

You: Taking things at your own pace might have felt more helpful?

Client: Yes. I know I'd have to make some effort, but it takes me a while to ... to unwind, I suppose.

You: Yes, I can see how important it would be for you to relax in the beginning – have some space to ... just to talk?

Client: Yes, that's it. That's right.

Going along this path with the client helps her to disclose some very useful pieces of information. She has identified shyness as a problem, then and now. She believes her life has improved somewhat. Already we have a problem focus and a sense that she experiences some hope. We learn that something has probably happened recently to set off an old pattern of behaviour. Most usefully, we discover that she didn't want to be rushed and still doesn't. (Perhaps she wasn't assertive enough in the past to tell her psychologist this!) As we elicit all this, we are also empathising, and in doing so we are beginning to form a therapeutic alliance. We do not wish to collude with any intention on the client's part to blame the psychologist. Rather, we wish to (1) get valuable information, (2) make links between previous experience of help attempts and the present, (3) demonstrate our concern for the client's welfare, (4) sensitise ourselves and the client to new hopes, and (5) tailor our counselling approach to the client's situation.

The key here is to encourage the client to spell things out. Push gently for more than vague answers. You want to know not just that a previous counselling experience was helpful or unhelpful, but how it was helpful or unhelpful, and beyond that you can ask how it could have been even more helpful. As you receive these answers you can begin to build up material for the kind of approach you will be using. If the client tells you, for example, that her previous counsellor talked about himself too much and that this was unhelpful, you will note this and watch any tendency you may have to do likewise. You can ask, in this example, what it was about the counsellor talking about himself too much that was off-putting. If, on the other hand, the client reports that her previous counsellor's self-disclosures made her feel more relaxed, you may decide to take note and do likewise. This kind of data-gathering helps you to formulate what has been called a kind of 'bespoke counselling', calculated to fit the client as elegantly as possible. Note, however, that if you learn that a previous counsellor offered much the same as you have to offer (and if you feel you cannot offer a significant variation on it) you may well consider making a referral.

Most of what we have said here applies equally to previous help offered by friends, partners, relatives, clergy and other people in the client's life. Whether such help has been given professionally or not, and was helpful or not (or came in shades of helpfulness and unhelpfulness) you can ask questions like these and gain valuable insights. In a pilot research project conducted by the authors, we put many such questions to a number of people, covering successful and unsuccessful experiences of counselling. We asked questions covering pre-counselling expectations, memories of first contacts with the counsellor, and many issues concerning the quality of understanding between counsellor and client. We framed the research around the idea of helpful and unhelpful aspects of counselling and psychotherapy. While everyone's experience is unique, and the good and bad vary enormously, all those interviewed, whether they had had successful or unsuccessful experiences, appeared to learn from the exercise – about themselves, their counsellors, and about the nature of help. We also discovered much, and therefore recommend such a research attitude to counsellors. You may rightly object that counselling is not research and that you have been trained not to ask too many questions! No, you are not a researcher as such, but you are client-centred and interested in giving clients of your best. We suggest that you do, therefore, need some of this information, and that you can obtain it sensitively without the client feeling that she is being interrogated.

* **Summary: Find out about your clients' previous helpful and unhelpful experiences of formal and informal counselling. Use this line of enquiry to build a picture of what the client will probably benefit and not benefit from. Do not offer more of the same bad experiences. Stress the dissimilarities between those**

**and what you intend to offer. Note and utilise elements of pre-
vious helpful experiences.**

11　Elicit the client's view of counselling and explain and demonstrate yours

Most people have some kind of preconception regarding counselling even if they cannot immediately articulate their views. One
of the commonest ideas is that counselling is a form of advice-
giving. Conversely, many people have heard that 'counsellors do
not tell you what to do'. Also, people may have in mind an 'as
seen on TV' version of what counselling will turn out to be. It
can conjure up pictures of couches, psychological assessments,
Rorschach tests, and therapists with diplomas hanging framed on
their walls as they sit smoking a pipe and looking piercingly at
their clients. In other words, clients can and do have all sorts of
expectations derived from various sources that may or may not
match the reality of seeing you.

'What do you imagine counselling is like?' you might ask. Your
client will then proceed to tell you, perhaps, some of the above.
'I expect you'll ask me about my childhood', she might say, or
'You probably want me to say whatever comes into my head'. If
you get these sorts of responses, what will you say? We advocate
a gently probing, exploratory approach. You might say, 'If I did
ask you about your childhood, would that help?' And you might
press the point further and ask how it would help. Now, what
you will also get as a response sometimes is the familiar 'I don't
know'. The client claims not to know what to expect from
counselling; she has no pictures in her mind at all. Try pressing
a little. 'What do you think it *could* be like?' you might venture
to ask. Another blank? Persist. Try this: 'Well, some people think
of counselling as a chance to reflect on their life, to take time out
and get a perspective on what's happened to them. But other
people have firm ideas about changing things they're very unhappy with now, so they want some action. Which of these means
more to you?' By working towards a focus you are likely to elicit
some specific ideas from the client.

The kinds of answers you receive not only may tell you a lot
about your client but also will be instructive for how you decide

to work. If your client says, 'Well, I know you're not going to tell me what to do', you may ask 'And are you happy with the idea that I may not tell you what to do?' thus eliciting information about her goals in coming for counselling. Another route forward from this kind of statement from a client is to consider explaining the way in which you work. This is, in fact, something we commend. It is helpful to think deeply about how you can describe the way you work, as a well-thought-out explanation can be therapeutic for some clients. Many clients, for example, are bewildered by the principle of 'abstinence' presented by some psychodynamic counsellors. If you do work psychodynamically, we suggest that you explain this to your client, simply but clearly. We strongly advocate that you respect the client's right as a consumer to know what she is 'buying'. Do not present counselling as a magical mystery tour! If your way of working involves giving plenty of space for exploration, for example, you might explain: 'Because I believe that you have your own answers within yourself, I prefer to give you time to stand back and look at yourself, and arrive at those answers in your own time; for that reason, I often leave many silences'. In saying this, you let the client know that silences are therapeutically purposeful, rather than disconcerting wastes of time.

Don't be afraid to give structure to your counselling sessions from the very beginning. There is a common belief in counselling that you must follow your client's material at all times. While it is true that the client's story is important, it is also important that the client is seeking counselling (not friendship) and that you are a counsellor, with some responsibilities towards your client. We believe that there is almost always a directive element in counselling and that it is advisable to recognise this and use it to help the client. Both clients and counsellors have preferences about the amount and kind of structuring in counselling, but it is better to face this issue squarely rather than to fudge it. Day and Sparacio (1989) outline the issues involved in structuring, including practical, ethical, methodological and philosophical considerations. When you are explaining your approach it is advisable to avoid jargon altogether. Use the language and concepts appropriate to your client. It is a highly instructive discipline to think over your work and theoretical stance in order to clarify your purposes and to test your ability to describe your service without mystification!

There is still the possibility that after discussions as those above, your client will still be unsure about what counselling is, whether it's what she wants and exactly what her goals are. If so, then the next step is to offer to demonstrate the process. 'Are you willing to agree to meet for, say, four of five sessions so that you can get the feel of how I work, and then you may be able to tell if it's right for you?' This demonstrates to the client that she is not making an irrevocable decision or spending a huge amount of money for a service she may regret paying for. She is paying as she goes and is free to decide that it is not for her. When you offer this way forward, be sure to remind the client that her goals and preferences are what are important. 'Some counsellors and clients are not the best match for each other, but by working together for a while, you'll be able to make up your mind about how well we work together', you might say. (As with the issue of tape-recording, by the way, it is important not to convey a message that is self-doubting and hence negatively self-fulfilling!) Show what you have to offer and demonstrate it well. Using brief explanations of your method of counselling, perhaps suggesting brief material to read on counselling, and allowing the client to experience it, all add up to an inviting beginning. These kinds of invitations and pieces of education are sometimes called 'role induction'. You need to decide for yourself how valuable they are both for your client and for yourself, but we recommend that you try them out.

* Summary: Discover what your clients expect counselling to be like. Consider how their expectations may colour the actual process. Be ready to give an account of how you work in clear, consumer-friendly language. Provide the beginnings of structuring. Give your client an 'introductory offer'.

12 Deal with practical agreements

We have already looked at confidentiality. There are certain other matters that have to be agreed before proceeding, and these are practical and business arrangements: scheduling, frequency of sessions, length of sessions, duration of counselling, and fees.

By scheduling, we mean the arrangements made concerning the times you will meet. Many counsellors and therapists like to offer a regular appointment time, for example, 4 pm every

Thursday. There are theoretical grounds for setting and maintaining a time that does not vary: it is thought to symbolise containment, reliability and safety for the client. If that is how you work, that's fine. Both of us prefer some flexibility in scheduling, for different reasons. Your own working life may be varied and regular meetings may not be possible. But you also may not believe (as we do not) that regularity is sacrosanct. Many clients are quite happy to make appointments from week to week, and it can even add to the working alliance between you when you negotiate mutually convenient times. Some clients definitely prefer appointments which are not in their working time, either so that they do not have to reveal that they are having counselling, or because they might lose money by taking time off work. We therefore advocate that you negotiate the best mutually agreed times.

Counselling is usually offered on a weekly basis. The reasons for this, apart from simple convention, probably lie in the identity of counselling as neither crisis intervention nor psychoanalysis. We believe that counselling focuses on recognisable problems, or clusters of problems or concerns, and has a problem-solving ethos. Brief counselling recognises the relatively small part it plays in the client's daily and ongoing life. It is one hour out of 168 hours in a client's week, and most of her obstacles and learning opportunities are to be encountered in her everyday life in the remaining 167 hours. So counselling may be conceived as the catalytic or the oasis hour. However, there is nothing sacrosanct about this weekly hour. At times you may want to fit in an extra session, for example if there is something particularly stressful going on in the client's life. Alternatively, you may decide on fortnightly meetings, or a changing pattern of frequency as the client improves. Budman and Gurman (1988) purposefully vary the frequency in order to emphasise the need for clients to confront issues in daily living. Overall, it is probably better to adhere to weekly sessions at least until you are sure of your way of working.

We have already alluded to a weekly hour. Some counsellors work to a full hour, but many work a fifty-minute hour. Nothing more is involved in this but practicalities. If you see one client after another, then you obviously need a short break between them (for a stretch, a sip of tea, a trip to the toilet, or in order to make a few notes). You may see each of your clients for a full hour and be able to schedule breaks as well. It depends entirely on where you work and what your workload is. Some counsellors see people for forty-five minutes. At the other end, some human-istic therapists prefer to offer longer sessions, sometimes of two hours. (This is the case, for example, with Mahrer (1989) and others who aim in their work at releasing deep feelings which may not fit neatly into fifty or sixty minutes.) These are matters for you to decide, but whatever your decision it is vital that you make it clear to your clients in advance. You may want to let your client know when there is, say, five minutes left at the end of a session. Our practice is to bring the session to a natural close and to terminate promptly but politely.

The question of the duration of counselling is rather more problematic. Sledge et al. (1990) compared time-limited therapy, brief therapy and long-term therapy. By time-limited therapy is meant a therapy contracted to last a pre-arranged, non-negotiable number of sessions (say, twelve) ending at a definite date. Brief therapy is defined in advance as lasting 'about three or four months' but no finishing date is set. Long-term or open-ended therapy is just that. (Interestingly, Sledge et al. found a drop-out rate from time-limited therapy that was half that of each of the other two.) We have outlined our views on brief counselling in our introduction. What is important here is the point that you decide what you are going to tell clients. You may have already explored their expectations or fantasies regarding the duration of counselling, but make these explicit agreements. There are some advantages to clear time limits. Clients can know in advance how much they will have to pay (if they are paying). They may find the notion of set limits more acceptable than an open-ended commitment. They may feel very contained by the time struc-ture. Also, many time-limited theorists argue that the finiteness of such counselling maximises commitment and discourages dependency on counselling (Ryle 1990).

What shall I charge? Every counsellor working privately must ask this question – and answer it! How do you decide? Rowan's (1989) rule of thumb is 'to charge fees which are high enough so that I don't feel exploited, and low enough so that I don't feel like an exploiter'. In practice, there is always a 'going rate' which you will know by asking around. The going rate varies according to the area in which you practise, your experience, any specialities, and so on. (We suggest that you consult the *Counselling and Psychotherapy Resources Directory*, which is published annually by the British Association for Counselling.) It is usual for coun-sellors to charge a little less when beginning, but there are no hard and fast rules. It may be true that if you charge too little you will arouse suspicions about your competency! Another consideration is your policy on reduced fees or a sliding scale. For political or humanitarian reasons, some counsellors offer one or two low-cost or even free places. Some offer a sliding scale (e.g. £1 per hour for every £1,000 of income) and some offer two or three fee bands for the client to choose from (e.g. £40, £30 or £20). There are advantages and disadvantages in each of these. Colin has learned from experience the pitfalls of wanting to offer the lowest possible deal. I found at one stage that I had several clients paying a minimum fee and that when I became freelance the earnings from these were not realistic. You need an overview of how much money you need to live on and what this means in terms of your realistic hourly fee. Equally, it is crucial that the client can afford counselling. Windy often says, 'I don't want to create financial problems for you at the same time as we're working to help you deal with your personal problems.'

You may well have debated with colleagues the merits of clients paying and not paying for counselling. There is a notion, with which neither of us agrees, that clients do not truly commit themselves to counselling if they receive it free. Orlinsky and Howard (1986) were unable to find any evidence to substantiate this idea. You may work in an agency which offers free counselling and which may or may not encourage donations. It probably is true for some clients that they feel uncomfortable 'taking without giving' but it is not true of all or even most human beings that payment increases commitment.

* **Summary: Make clear agreements about when you will meet, how often, and over what period. Negotiate suitable mutual arrangements. Consider, discuss and agree to fees, again taking into account your needs and your clients' ability to pay.**

PART II
Assessing the client's concerns

13 Allow the client to talk

One of the features of counselling which distinguishes it from everyday conversation is the quality of listening. Many people seek counselling precisely because there is no one in their life with whom they can speak and hope to be attended to without constant interruptions. Most counsellors are acutely aware of this because counsellor training courses devote a lot of time to developing active listening skills. These skills, as you will know, include empathic responding. You give your client plenty of space, but you also communicate your interest and understanding. So when clients come into counselling and begin to tell you their life story, it is entirely appropriate to hear them out. It may be the first time they have had the opportunity to feel really heard. In giving you their story, they are doing at least two things. One is the giving of information – their history, circumstances and feelings about all of it. Another is the process of unburdening, which can be in itself cathartic and therapeutic. Don't, then, underestimate the importance and power of letting clients talk from their frame of reference.

Now, clients vary enormously. Some like to talk a lot and need little prompting. Some will talk about their whole life. Others will talk specifically about a current pressing problem. Some will talk effusively but aimlessly, perhaps out of embarrassment or avoidance. Some clients simply have a style of talking that is unfocused and rambling. So we do not want to give you the idea that you must let all clients talk at great length without interruption. You need to be sensitive to the nuances involved and you are faced with a seeming paradox: how do you allow clients to talk, as we suggest, while at the same time deciding when talk is cathartic and useful, or defensive or rambling? In the case of someone who is genuinely and acutely distressed you will instinctively listen without a need to intervene. In the case of someone who is trying with difficulty to disclose significant information, your ability to respond empathically is a key skill, but you will also need to initiate some subtle structuring. Egan (1990) writes about the counsellor's role in 'helping clients tell their stories'. He suggests that clients frequently display either *choice* or *change* issues. People may be aware of choices in front of them but may not feel ready to act. Others may desire changes in their lives but not know how to begin. Egan advocates that you be flexible, collaborative and action-oriented. Facilitate your client's need to talk, but give some shape to it too. From the very beginning you will be making an assessment (even if this is intuitive and informal) and part of this is to ask yourself if the client's needs are initially or primarily for catharsis, for relationship-building with you, or for gaining clarity and problem-identification.

A word on assessment. If your way of working involves taking a history of all clients, we do urge you to be ready to put this aside when it is obvious that your client is distressed or anxious. Also, do not pepper clients with the kinds of questions we have listed here if they are distressed. Allow time. Now, it is sometimes the case that your client is prepared for change, has a specific problem in mind, and may need neither a lot of time to talk nor a lengthy assessment. In such cases you would be well advised to meet clients on their problem-solving ground. In allowing clients time to talk (say, in most of the first session or sessions) you are learning their style of presentation and dynamics, and you are formulating a working hypothesis. But you may need to do little of this if the client comes with a specific goal and wants to get on with it!

Let's return to the client who rambles. If you are afraid that to interrupt is to break the client's momentum or to impose your own frame of reference, do disabuse yourself of this notion. When a client persistently talks without any focus or affect, we advocate that you do indeed interrupt. Let's look at a possible dialogue:

Client: Well I was at my mother's last Wednesday, or was it Thursday, and I said to her (she's always doing something else when you talk to her) that I was thinking of moving away. I don't know if I want to move too far into the country or not – I might feel isolated, but I'm fed up with the city, the muggings and pollution, you know – and maybe I'll just look for somewhere a bit quieter. The thing about my mother is that she's always put me down. I know I can't blame her, that's wrong, isn't it? She says she hates the city too.

You: I just need to see if I'm understanding you. You've told me rather a lot. I gather that you're not altogether happy with your mother or with where you live. Is that right?

Client: Yes. Well, only last week a man was burgled in my street and had all his stereo equipment taken. It's terrible. I was just saying to my sister . . .

You: If I may, I'd like to try and focus on one or two things a little more closely. Can you remind me what it was that made you want counselling?

Client: Well, the doctor says I'm depressed and I need to talk about it.

You: The doctor thinks you're depressed. Your mother, you say, has always put you down. I'd like to know how you feel yourself?

This client may have a certain conversational style that is sprawling, or she may be anxiously defensive. But unless stopped and guided into some focused concerns, she may ramble on indefinitely. If you allow her to, she may well waste her time and money. She may also get quite the wrong impression of counselling and may *need* to have someone help her to focus. This kind of interruption isn't rudeness and it isn't against the rules of counselling! On the contrary, it is sensitive to the underlying feelings of the client and it firmly establishes the idea that counselling is not just an everyday chit-chat but a purposeful and sometimes confrontative exercise.

All that we have said here about letting the client talk, while empathising and structuring, implies that you respond to the client from her frame of reference. You may have a particular theory of counselling and a hypothesis about this client, but your task, especially in early sessions, is to communicate to the client your understanding of her frame of reference. This means that you need to be able to relax enough to be truly with the client. Some beginning counsellors, naturally enough, are anxious about how they are performing. You may be acutely aware of all your trainers' admonitions, which can lead to self-consciousness. You may be tape-recording your work and anticipate a supervisor hearing it. This can get you into a frame of mind called 'spectatoring' in which you are anxiously watching your own counselling performance. This can easily remove you from your client's frame of reference. Accept that this can happen, it's quite common and it's only human. Don't beat yourself up over it. If you catch yourself at it during a session, just be aware of it and let it go. Bring yourself back into the frame of reference of your client. If necessary, ask the client to repeat something, rather than risk making yourself even more anxious about missing some vital piece of information!

The point about knowing and responding to the client's frame of reference is that you need to be attuned to the content and feeling so that you can initiate movement forward. You listen for the 'leading edge' in what the client conveys. What is most important or urgent in what she says? To which themes does she most often return? What makes her excited, breathless or flat? At which moments does she blush, sigh, become silent or loud? Be immersed in the client's world and respond as far as you can from her viewpoint. You may note that you have a tendency to want to reflect statements back, a kind of technical, empty reflecting; this may be a sign that you are spectatoring and don't want to risk getting things wrong. This frequently occurs with beginning counsellors, so don't worry. However, the more that you can let this go and immerse yourself in the client's phenomenal world, the better. But don't demand that you must not spectate, because if you do, you will do it all the more!

* Summary: Let your clients unburden themselves, tell their story and benefit from catharsis. Interrupt if necessary to prevent rambling. Begin to lend structure to what is happening. Allow yourself to enter and to respond from the client's frame of reference.

---

14   Listen for and respond to the problems, not the story

We have said that the client's story is important. However, we need to remind ourselves that in brief counselling it is not an appropriate task to gather exhaustively every biographical detail. You will hear, in each story, certain themes or problems which stand out from the narrative. These may include, for example, losses, interpersonal conflicts, need for approval, or moral crises. They may be obvious or not, and they may be centre stage or perhaps they will appear and disappear, but your ear will pick them up. We believe it is more appropriate in this way of working to identify such themes rather than to keep an open agenda or to slowly note the many latent themes in the client's story. Look back at Section 3 ('why now?') to see the significance of dealing with what is presented at this time rather than attempting an omnipotent once-and-for-all cure.

You may want to distinguish between a background biographical matrix and the themes emerging in counselling. Beyond that, you can identify specific problems within themes. For example:

Client: It's always been this way for me, it's always been a struggle. Somehow I knew when I went for this job that I wasn't going to get it.

You: You've had these disappointments before and this is another one – it was almost inevitable.

Client: Yeah. I mean, I tried. I'm well qualified and I put my case well, but somehow . . . I suppose at my age, somehow I'm not on target. There are younger people around.

You: From all you've told me, it seems that you're angry at being left out, left behind. You know you've got what it takes, yet you're also aware that it doesn't come across, and your age is getting to you. Is that it?

Client: Yes. As I said, there's something familiar about this, but at the same time I have changed and I do want things now, but I feel penalised.

You: I'd like you to tell me more about the 'struggle', but also about your present circumstances and why you are putting pressure on yourself to seek promotion. Would it be a good idea, too, to look at exactly how you do present yourself at an interview?

We might infer from this piece of dialogue that the client has an underlying self-sabotaging pattern of behaviour and beliefs. But the counsellor decides not to explore (or re-explore) these in depth. He wants to move into the present day, to what brought the client into counselling now, and he asks for a concrete account of how the client conducts himself. In this way the counsellor tapers the client's concerns into workable material. We do not deny that any client's past influences his present experience, and there is indeed a place for exploring significant personal history. But if you aim to be effective in a relatively short time, and if you believe that counselling (and therapy) tends to be shorter, by design or default, than we might like it to be, then you need to separate meaningful and mobilising information from other (interesting but not necessarily usable) details.

* Summary: Pick out prevalent themes in the client's story. In collaboration with the client, identify particular problems emerging from these themes, and focus on examples that can provide therapeutic leverage.

---

15   Ask for any crucial or helpful
information

Depending on your training, orientation and personal preferences
you may use a formal assessment procedure or not. Even if you
disapprove of formal assessments, as some counsellors do, we
consider that there are certain items of information it is crucial
to know.

It is widely acknowledged, for example, that if someone has
a serious drinking problem it is probably useless to try doing
any counselling until that problem is under control. Therefore, if
you suspect (or even if you do not suspect) that your client has
such a problem, ask about it. There are degrees of addiction to,
or occasional abuse of, alcohol and drugs. Ask about the use of
substances in detail if necessary, whether these are prescribed or
not, legal or not. The point about getting such information is
that if you proceed with counselling while your client is abusing
such substances, time may be wasted, the client's honesty and
moods may be affected, and you may suffer as a result. It would
be appropriate to refer a client in these circumstances to a specialist form of treatment, although you might offer to see them
once they had their primary problem under control.

Another crucial piece of information concerns the risk of suicide.
If there is any sign of severe depression, such as hopelessness
coupled with agitation, lack of supportive friendships, and so on,
then you should definitely find out more about the client's frame
of mind and the resources available to him. This is one of those
areas in which counsellors are sometimes uncomfortable. 'But if
I mention it, it just might put the idea in her head', is one fairly
typical worry. The chances are that if you experience a concern
for your client's mental stability, both of you will be relieved to
have it aired. If there is a discussion about suicidal ideation,
make it specific, including questions about previous attempts,
her precise plans to take her own life, social support systems, and
medical or psychiatric assessments. You may decide on the basis
of the replies you get that you do not want to take on this client.
If so, it is essential that you effect a referral in a way that does
not further discourage your already demoralised client. Ensure
that the client knows telephone numbers of the Samaritans or
Social Services. Stewart (1989) believes strongly in the need
to confront these issues and to make contracts in regard to

them. His strategy for 'blocking tragic outcomes' involves careful history-taking and analysis of ego states and scripts. Your strategy may be more informal, but you are advised to think about it and to address these subjects with clients without embarrassment, but with due sensitivity.

Apart from the subject of suicide, there are other matters that are important to consider. Since we are aware that different counsellors find different kinds of information crucial or helpful, we include a list of some common questions:

1 What are your social circumstances? (Family? Friends?)
2 What are your financial circumstances? (Employed? Solvent?)
3 What are your living conditions? (Homeless? Poorly housed?)
4 Do you have any current illnesses? (Physical or mental?)
5 Have you had any major illnesses or accidents?
6 Are you currently using any medication or substances?
7 Do you drink, smoke or overeat?
8 Have you been involved in any criminal activity?
9 Are you receiving any help from other professionals?
10 Have there been any major losses or separations in your life?

Some clients are pleased to be asked such questions because they may fit their expectations of a medical model of being helped; they may convey a sense of detailed interest in the client; and they will often elicit information that may not be volunteered by the client otherwise. What you ask will depend on your model of counselling and also on any requirements of the agency you may work in. If you place great emphasis on support networks you may be concerned to know a lot about these. If you have a particularly psychosomatic orientation, then you may well want to know about previous illnesses. (Some counsellors, as a matter of course, ask clients for the name and address of their GP.) It is up to you whether you elicit this kind of information gradually and tactfully, or formally at the outset, or even not at all. Think about what you need to know and why you need to know it. When you are working quite specifically on a focal concern, then this may dictate what you need to know. If you feel that certain questions are an intrusion of privacy, and not relevant for counselling purposes, don't ask them. If you believe that the more information you have, the better, then explain this to the client before asking. (Bear in mind, however, that it is possible to amass an awful lot of useless information!) If your client arrives in distress, you will probably not ask these kinds of questions at that time (unless you work in certain settings which require the information).

* **Summary: If it is appropriate to the way you work, have prepared the kinds of question you will ask to elicit crucial or helpful information. What in the client's life may be detrimental to counselling? Decide in particular what your policy is on suicidal ideation, alcoholism and other life-threatening areas.**

---

16   Establish the reflection process

Something that we recommend you do from the outset is to establish as a norm the practice of asking for feedback on counselling sessions. You have already prepared the ground for this in some of the previous questions here. Let the client know that you value her comments and that you want to be as helpful as possible. How does she feel about the counselling relationship? How can you encourage her to feel and act like an equal partner (or to feel 'taken care of' if that seems initially more appropriate for a particular client)? The reflection process occurs when both client and counsellor step back from the content of the counselling to look at how well the alliance between them is holding. Bordin (1979) argued that the therapeutic alliance consists of bonds, goals and tasks. We have both found in our work that sensitive but explicit discussion with clients about the therapeutic relationship, agreed goals and mutually understood ways of working towards those goals, helps to raise difficulties before they escalate into irreparable misunderstandings or breakdowns in communication. Furthermore, the practice of encouraging an ongoing reflection on the work helps to keep it on course. Your willingness to hear regularly from the client about her views of the counselling process is likely to increase the bond between you.

   Questions you might ask to elicit this kind of feedback include 'How do you feel about being here?' 'How do you feel about me?' 'How do you feel about what we did today?' 'Is there anything I said today that was confusing?' 'What has been most helpful about the sessions so far?' 'Are we addressing the issues that are important for you?' Such questions give permission to the client to be critical, to speak openly and to reflect on the process. They encourage a working alliance, a sense of you and the client working together in the same direction. They also serve to demythologise counselling.

* **Summary: Get into the habit of asking for comments on how counselling is going from the client's point of view. Encourage the client to voice any doubts about your relationship, about your way of working and the goals towards which you are working with them. Integrate this into your work.**

---

17   Identify the client's stage of change

We now want to look more closely at the idea of identifying stages of change according to the model presented by Prochaska and DiClemente (1984). The four main stages are pre-contemplation, contemplation, action and maintenance. Here we shall focus on those stages involving contemplation and beyond because the pre-contemplation stage is very problematic. People in the pre-contemplation stage regard themselves as not having a problem, or not having a serious enough problem to worry about, or as being able to cope without changing anything. Often such people have come to a counsellor because they've been sent or coerced. They come grudgingly and are clearly not prepared for actual change. If you do work with them, you will need to build trust and to establish that it is their perception of any problems you are interested in (not their family's, for example) and that you are willing to spend time discussing counselling, and its pros and cons, in relation to their doubts. If you decide not to work with pre-contemplators (and some counsellors do decide not to) then you might offer to see them at a later stage, should they feel ready for counselling. Don't be judgemental of their hesitancy, mistrust or disowning of problems.

When people are in the contemplation stage they are actively wondering about change, thinking it might be a good thing, vaguely wishing for greater clarity in regard to problems, or imagining that someone will be able to tell them what to do. Now, the important thing to remember is to tailor your interventions so as to join clients in the stage they are at. If people are contemplators, it is inadvisable to treat them as if they are pre-contemplative, doubtful and resistant. Equally, you would not treat them as being 'ready to go', that is in the action stage. The most appropriate counselling mode with contemplators is the exploratory one. Understand the clients' questions and hopes and elicit their expectations. Help them to feel understood. Provide the climate in which their confidence in the counselling (and personal growth) process will grow.

Should your client be in the action stage, you will need to adjust yourself to this. Someone may enter counselling with you having already worked on some problems. They may have already thought things through, they may understand their own dynamics or know clearly what they want to do. They are ready to act and may feel impatient with further exploration. Don't make the mistake of regarding this attitude as clients' defensive refusal to examine themselves in depth! There may be such subtleties involved, but we advocate in brief counselling that you address the client's presented concerns until they (perhaps) turn out to be something else! So if your client says. 'I think what I need to do is find another job', don't immediately see this as escapism or as symbolic of something else. Investigate it. 'I'd like to know something about your present job and what kind of job you'd prefer', perhaps followed by, 'Tell me what you've done in the direction of finding another job', is more appropriate in this stage of change than, say, 'Are you sure that's what you want? When people are in turmoil, it's often a better idea not to change things around until we're more settled inside'. Don't deny the client's reality. This is not the same as suppressing all your instincts if you feel that such a client is operating on a fantasy of a better life through a different job. Begin with the client's reality.

We shall not go into the maintenance stage in much depth. Obviously clients will have done considerable work on self-change if they have already thought through a problem and made changes. Someone may come to you in this stage in order to get some reinforcement. Someone who has overcome an addiction, for example, may at times feel troubled by old cravings and seek a means of expressing this and gaining support. He may also be looking for new strategies. Recognise this and work with these concerns. You certainly should not have to go back to square one with such clients.

This last point is crucial. While recognising the stages of change takes practice, and may never be 'scientific', we believe it sharpens your skills considerably if you are aware of them. But it does have implications. If you are wedded to a single therapeutic theory and you want to apply it to all clients, difficulties will arise. In practice, most counsellors do adapt their style to each client. But if, for example, you work with a pure model of person-centred counselling, you may well have trouble with clients who come in for help already in the action stage. People who have found the motivation to do something to change their life, perhaps to make specific decisions or to give up an addictive habit, are likely to want action strategies and reinforcement for them. They have been through the contemplative stage. If you insist on further contemplation at this point you may lose the client or delay their progress unnecessarily. We are not suggesting that you must master half a dozen theories and many more techniques, but we do advocate flexibility. If you work behaviourally, or cognitive-behaviourally, and you prefer a brisk pace in counselling, you will do a disservice to a client who is hovering nervously between pre-contemplation and contemplation. Such a client needs time and support. Having the stages of change model in mind will help you to make rapid adjustments of style and intervention.

What may not be obvious is that clients can, in presenting two or three problems, be at different stages of change with each of them. Recognising this requires extra awareness and adaptability.

Let us suppose that your client mentions problems with assertiveness, with trying new activities and with the loss of a boyfriend. You may regard these as all one problem stemming from early experiences of attachment and separation anxiety. Within a brief counselling contract, however, in which you are aiming to be as effective as possible, we think you need to focus. The client mentions three areas she wishes to work on. Don't impose your view, if you have one, that these all relate to early material that needs long-term regressive work to correct. We come on to the prioritising of concerns in guideline 23. Here, the task for you is to decide, with the client, at what stage she is with each problem.

Let's say that she split up from her boyfriend a year ago and that she has cried about it, thought through it, but still misses him. Together you may decide that she has grieved substantially for the loss of her relationship and is in a maintenance stage of accepting the reality of it. An appropriate counselling approach may be to help her to express her feelings about her boyfriend in depth when necessary and encourage her to accept the loss. She wants to fill up some time; this relates to losing her boyfriend but also to realistic wishes for personal development at this stage in her life. Perhaps she is contemplative with regard to moving on substantially in her life, in which case you may help her to do some long-term planning when appropriate. However, she reveals that she specifically wants to join a language class now, and she identifies a need to be assertive in relation to this. Here she is clearly ready for action. You meet her action stage with appropriate, well-defined change strategies, for example assertiveness training techniques and identifying and disputing irrational beliefs about the need to feel comfortable in new situations. Remember that clients may spend a lot of time on one problem and little on another, and that may be entirely appropriate.

To help you identify the stages of change, a questionnaire is included (Appendix 1). This will sharpen your own practice. You may decide to use it with clients. If you do, it can be used generally for assessment, or in a more detailed way to identify the stages of change for each problem a client presents.

* Summary: Consider integrating the stages of change model into your work. Learn to discern the stages of change your clients are at with each of their problems. Learn to adapt your style and your interventions accordingly.

---

18   Encourage the client's involvement in the process

It is well established that counselling works better from the clients' point of view when they feel involved and consulted. We advocate that from the outset you encourage this kind of involvement. This means that you need to ensure that clients understand the tasks required of them in counselling. 'Tasks' is a word it is easy to misunderstand. By tasks is meant those activities that are necessary for the client and counsellor to engage in, and to understand the purpose of, in order to optimise therapeutic progress. Some counselling approaches see progress as implicit and tasks as an alien (behavioural) concept. This is not the case. Ursano et al. (1991) summarise the tasks of a patient in psychodynamic psychotherapy as

1   developing a working alliance with the therapist
2   learning free association

3   appreciating the atmosphere of safety
4   recognising the disappointment of the opening phase
5   developing an understanding of transference, defence and
    resistance
6   learning how to work with dreams.

It cannot be assumed that clients have read all about a certain
method or that they will pick it up by intuition or telepathy. Let
them know your therapeutic intentions. Explain the value of
your methods. Seek collaboration.

Whatever your preferred way of working, your clients always
have tasks. These are more obvious, perhaps, in cognitive-
behavioural counselling, where clients are asked to do homework, and in sessions are actively encouraged to produce
examples of their thinking processes. In Gestalt counselling, the
client has the task of getting in touch with the 'boundaries' of
her experience. In person-centred counselling, clients have the
tasks of engaging in the process of self-exploration, learning to
trust themselves and their own thinking and feeling processes.
We believe much counselling would be improved if counsellors
of different persuasions would explain these matters to their
clients and seek their collaboration, instead of assuming that
clients will guess what their tasks are or naturally fit in with
what is going on. If client participation is as crucial as we suggest,
then anything which fails to deal with client passivity invites
problems in counselling. You may object that come clients are
characterologically passive, and if this is the case you are advised
to consider either referral or negotiating a long-term therapeutic
contract with them. But sometimes clients appear passive because they are mystified about counselling, and rightly so if they
are expected to guess what it's all about.

One of the pitfalls of working with passive clients is the
temptation to do the work for them, for example by talking a lot.
The problem here is that the more you do this, the more you
reinforce their passivity. Refrain from falling into this trap. The
opposite trap is to become persecutory, of course – perhaps trying
to out-stare or out-silence your client. A better way, we believe,
is to explore and gently challenge passivity, for example 'It seems
you're finding it extremely difficult to let go enough to talk about
what's really upsetting you.' 'It's been found that counselling
works best when people are ready to take a few risks, however
small. Is there anything you're close to risking?', would be an
attempted lever. You can also reinforce what change attempts

clients do make, however small, in order to establish a pattern of active involvement. Approaches like Ryle's (1990) cognitive-analytic therapy are built around the expectation of 'active participation', employing a variety of self-reporting questionnaires and letter-writing tasks.

* **Summary: Convey the expectation that counselling requires active involvement on the part of the client. Discourage passivity and avoid the traps of leaving your clients to guess what their tasks are, or performing them for them.**

---

19   Use appropriate language and pacing

Clients, as we have said and as you will know, differ enormously. Person-centred counselling underlines the uniqueness of clients. One of the ways in which uniqueness is expressed is language. Class differences in Britain are still fairly obvious and are betrayed in people's accents. In an increasingly multicultural society the use of language becomes even more complex, rich and open to misunderstanding. Let's look at some basics.

Some people prefer formal language. By this we mean that some clients will address you as Mr, Mrs, Ms or Dr rather than by your first name. They may also talk about themselves or people in their lives in formal terms. This may be simply a preference, a cultural norm or a defensive style. Whatever it is, you will do well to note it and to adapt your own language so that it is not, initially, too dissonant. It would not be helpful for me to respond to a new client who calls me Dr Dryden as 'mate', for example. On the other hand, a client who readily and naturally calls you by your first name will probably find you rather stiff if you respond by calling her Mrs Brown throughout sessions. Respect for clients does not mean that you should be overly formal. It is quite in order to ask clients how they prefer to be addressed and to tell them your preference.

There are degrees of formal and informal language. Some people, in their everyday lives, swear a lot, and may swear in their counselling sessions. If you are uncomfortable with swearing (or particular forms of swearing) this is something to think about. With those people to whom liberal expletives come naturally, you are more likely to form a good working alliance if you can either join them in such language or at least feel comfortable with it. We are not suggesting that you put on a phoney cockney accent and play a part. You will want to be as true to yourself as possible. But if it is apparent that you are from a very different class or culture, the communication between you and your client may become difficult. One way of dealing with this is to notice the client's non-verbal reactions to you. Another is to incorporate into your reflection process with clients questions about your differing styles. 'People do have different ways of saying things and I wonder if we're always on the same wavelength here or not? How well do you think we're communicating with each other?' or 'Have you found anything that I have said off-putting?'

Some people have a very dry and stiff style of relating and may well bring this manner into counselling. You may adapt to it or question it (if it seems to be part of the client's problem). But you may also find it useful at times to introduce humour and colour into the language used between you. This can give permission to the client to do likewise. Experiment with imagery that may evoke feelings. Do all of this gradually and experimentally. Does the client respond? Are there particular forms of language that get through to the client where others don't? This can work the other way too. If a client has a hysterical manner (speaking dramatically, shrilly, speedily, for example) it would not help for you to mirror this for too long! You can influence the client, bring her down, as it were, into a way of talking that is calm enough to initiate effective counselling. What we hope these examples show is that there are no black and white prescriptions, but there are indications for adjusting your language to strengthen the bond between you and to help the client move subtly from one mood to another. Working congruently, you can infer which kind of language style will be more effective.

A note on jargon. In almost all cases, avoid it. Technical language is appropriate, perhaps, as professional shorthand with colleagues. But when working with clients, use their language. Avoid, on the whole, diagnostic terms and psychological terms. (If you are using certain approaches like transactional analysis, where counselling depends on teaching basic concepts from the model, then you obviously will use technical language, but only after you have carefully explained it.) Another kind of jargon is 'I hear what you're saying'. Which can be very jarring. Some clients (Colin has been one of them) can be easily put off if they sense this kind of stylised language. Attend to the client and you will pick up whether or not you are striking the right notes. The wrong notes can also, of course, yield interesting reactions, but in the beginning aim for an alliance, not a negative transference–countertransference battle.

Clients are unique in their pacing too. But so are counsellors. The manner in which we process information, both conceptual and personal (emotional) varies a lot. We all speak and think at different speeds. The most problematic scenario, probably, is one in which a very 'slow' counsellor is working with a very 'fast' client. There are reasons for thinking that it is easier for counsellors to slow themselves down than to hurry themselves up. Now, we are not saying that you must anxiously attempt to adapt upwards or downwards to your client's pace. But note it. And go with it rather than against it. Clients will be put off if they feel you're hurrying them, and they may also feel exasperated if they feel they're several steps ahead of you. What we're saying here presupposes that a client's pace is not a pathological manifestation, like a 'hurry up' driver. But even if it is, your first task will be to meet the client rather than to pathologise her.

So what if a client is, say, very slow in delivering her ideas? How do you respond? Remember the reflection process. 'I notice that you're taking quite a time to think about your answers. Is that the way you usually think and respond, and is it valuable for you?' What you are after is information and leverage. The client may say, 'I don't know. I've never thought about it. I think I am a bit unused to this situation, but yes, I'm generally on the slow side.' You can then investigate this further, according to the focus in counselling. But at a working level, it may imply that you had better accept it, rather than become impatient and cause the client to become anxious.

* Summary: Be sensitive to the client's uniqueness in relation to language use. Adapt your own responses as far as you can, allowing yourself to be more or less informal. Avoid jargon. Be sensitive to the client's pace and adjust to it.

---

20   Use your influence base appropriately

Many counsellors believe that to set out to influence clients in any way is an ultimate transgression. It is still the case that some counsellors bend over backwards in an effort (mistakenly, in our opinion) not to convey any direction to their clients whatsoever. It has been shown that even Carl Rogers delivered his 'hmmms' and 'ahas' in a manner that revealed a subtle pattern of differential reinforcement. You may want to think carefully about this, but we feel that it is an unavoidable fact in counselling that you do wield influence. Indeed, Ivey et al. (1987) define counselling and therapy as 'processes of personal influence'.

One way of looking at this is as follows. Clients are often influenced (depending on their personalities) either by the perceived expertness or the perceived attractiveness of their counsellors. In a similar vein some clients will respond more favourably to the formality of their counsellors, but others to a more informal style. Expertness is evident in professional qualifications, training and knowledge, and the setting or area in which you work. Expertness often, but not invariably, goes together with formality. Attractiveness is evident in the counsellor's personality, warmth and appearance and it often goes together with informality. Windy has given before (Dryden 1991: 112) the example of how I adjusted my manner from formal to informal when seeing first, a client wanting a formal counsellor, and second, a client appreciating a much more informal style of counselling. This adjustment included my removing my tie and joining my second client in a drink of Coke, while we both had our feet up on the table. This was not done mechanically or phonily. It was, however, done by design. I was able to do this genuinely because I am able to range from being formal to becoming informal quite easily.

As a beginning counsellor you are unlikely to be able to call so much on the 'expert' with which to influence your clients. (You may well, however, have expertness in related fields which you may emphasise.) Good therapeutic bonds are established with counsellors-in-training, for example, when clients warm to their enthusiasm, alertness and even vulnerability. 'I'm a counsellor-in-training and I'm looking forward to working with you' introduces you better than an apologetic or defensive 'I'm just a trainee counsellor and I have to get some experience'! If you are confronted with clients who clearly prize expertness, you might present them with areas in which you do have some expertise. Or you might consider making a referral. But remember how much clients differ, and that many clients will feel reassured by your accepting manner rather than your white coat! (It is important not to mislead your client as to your qualifications, but equally it is unnecessary and unhelpful (in our view) to present your lack of experience and qualifications in great detail.)

Other ways in which formality and informality are evident include the use of humour and the offering of refreshments. Freudians may be aghast at both these suggestions, but there are many counsellors (and psychotherapists) who welcome clients with a cup of tea, and freely engage in humour. What is your preferred style? And perhaps more importantly, how flexible are you in varying your style of relating? You can always try to find out which of these practices are helpful and which are not by asking your clients in the reflection process.

* **Summary: Consider the fact that you will influence your clients, whether it is conscious or not, and whether you like it or not. How can you use this knowledge to improve your service to individual clients? How comfortable are you in adjusting your style? If you are a beginner, accept this and use it beneficially.**

21 Be sensitive to important client differences

Clients have different expectations about how their counsellors will act. Richert (1983) divides clients into 'medical modellers' (who expect a high level of authority); 'revelationists' (who look for a powerful and penetrative counsellor); 'problem-solvers' (who want, not so much authority, as technical application from their counsellors); and 'explorers' (who seek a non-authoritarian, fellow-traveller kind of counsellor). Can you detect such different tastes in your clients? And if you can, what do you do about it?

We have advocated an attitude of flexibility throughout this book, and it applies here very powerfully. If you accept a need to identify counselling styles that will best help your clients, then whether you follow a schema like Richert's, or your own intuition, this has certain implications. If you are someone who, as a counsellor, likes to be a fellow explorer, and you have a client who clearly wants to look up to you and get some answers, will you spend weeks trying to break down his 'external frame of reference' before going on to address the problems with which he came in the first place? Certainly some counsellors do work this way. But if you accept the value of a focal approach, and the likelihood of a relatively brief time with your client, you will want to capitalise on clues your clients give you.

Howard et al. (1987) have their own view of client differences. This attempts to match client readiness for change with appropriate styles of counselling from the counsellor. Supporting, teaching, delegating and telling are the main styles identified by these writers. Without going too much into detail, we want to raise the point that this schema too suggests a need for flexibility from counsellors. We don't want you to think you have to enrol in acting classes to prepare yourself for your next counselling session. But we are saying that having *one* invariant, relational stance towards your clients is unlikely to be sufficient. Arnold Lazarus uses the term 'authentic chameleon' for this requirement to adjust to each client. Counselling is, after all, not simply a case of being true to yourself, but also of being true to and useful to your client. You may not always be conscious of choices, but throughout your work you are faced with choices of adaptation. It is your task, we suggest, to do the adjusting to your clients, rather than their job to meet you on your ground. There may be times when you can't find the required responses within your repertoire. At these times, supervision is, of course, crucial. And, at the end of the day, referral is always an option.

* Summary: Clients differ. They expect different things from their counsellors. You can maximise your effectiveness by recognising differences and by trying to adjust your style. Don't stay in the same mode all the time.

22 Use an appropriate degree of structure

By structure here, we mean the kind of framework you give to your work with clients. Once they are engaged in counselling and somewhat familiar with their tasks, they will need, depending on their personalities and defences, variable styles of containment.

Let's look at an example of an 'all over the place', 'hysterical' kind of client:

Client: She just won't stop making that noise with her records and I've told her dozens of times, if I have to tell her again . . . Why do I have to put up with up this, can you tell me? Oh, I do go on, don't I? It's not as if . . . Why should I have to take it?! It's the same at work with that stupid secretary. Sometimes I think I'd be better off out of it all. Maybe I need a holiday. Do you think I need a holiday? I wish I could just decide something and get on with it!

You: Let me stop you a moment. I'm not sure where you're going. We started off talking about your neighbour. Now, try to tell me again the main problem area for you.

Client: Main problem?! Ha! Sometimes I don't know if I'm coming or going! If it isn't one thing, it's another.

You: There may be a lot of things, but you can only deal with one thing at a time. Now, which of these are you most upset about at this time?

If your client still goes from one topic to another, ask her permission for you to interrupt her. Having obtained this permission, and if the occasion arises again, interrupt politely but firmly. This may be hard work, but it is necessary. This client may be trying hard to keep to the task of looking at a particular problem area, but the task slips away. It is your task to do the reminding, the interrupting, the guiding back into the agreed task. This is what a structure means. It involves an initial agreement, but also maintenance of that agreement. Sometimes in cases like this it may mean a degree of forcefulness. You may need to drive home a single point. But you may need to initiate a strategy of ordering, of encouraging the client progressively to look at things in an unfamiliar, sequential manner.

Let's consider another kind of client – someone who is rather obsessive, or 'uptight':

You: So you agree that you'd like to be able to relax more around the house?

Client: Yes. Relax. I want to. But it isn't easy. I'm sorry. I'm trying. But it isn't easy. I just can't stand to see things untidy. I have to do something about it.

You: I notice, Mary, that you always sit very upright when you're here. Pretty stiff and uncomfortable-looking. Would you like to be able to relax more here?

Client: (Wringing hands) Well . . . well, I, yes, I know I'm not relaxed, but, but that's how I always am, Mrs Jones.

You: I'd like to hear you call me Christine, and maybe sit back in that chair, instead of leaning forward. Will you try that?

Client: I . . . you mean now? Call you Christine now? Lean back?

Your task here is to help loosen the client up. This may take some time and you may try various strategies, but they will all be part of a structure in which you have the client's welfare at heart. You won't use the same structure for all clients. In fact, you will always use slightly different kinds and degrees of structure with different clients. By forming ongoing and adjusting 'diagnostic impressions' of clients, you will begin to feel what is required by each one at various times in the counselling process. And referring back to the reflection process, asking the client if what you've done is helpful, will help you to fine-tune the structure.

* **Summary: Depending on the kind of client, you will decide how highly structured or 'loosely' structured the sessions might be. Get impressions of what your clients require to find a working shape in their counselling.**

---

23   Prioritise concerns and select a target concern

You will have become aware of what your client's concerns are, perhaps in a vague or shifting way. What you need to do now is to address concretely the client's concerns in order to prioritise them. We think this is important because, if you don't do it, you run the risk of talking at cross purposes. Your client may be trying to work on one issue while you are steadfastly referring back to another. So be sure that you arrive at an agreement as to what the concerns are and how they are ranked in the client's mind.

How can you help the client to decide on priorities? First, consider the severity of problems. Your client may be vaguely discontented with her job, be bulimic, and unassertive. Now, these may or may not be connected. (Some theorists argue that everything is connected, and it may be, but within a brief counselling perspective you are not groping around in the depths of the psyche hoping that eventually everything will fall into place.) Let's suppose that the issue of bulimia is the severest problem at this time. If you and the client agree on this, and you agree that severity is the criterion you will use to decide on priorities, then you can go ahead and work on this concern.

Second, remember the client's choice of concerns. She may be quite clear that what she wants to focus on is her relationship with her father. You may, let's say, not agree with her view (she may show signs of avoiding some anxiety-inducing situation in her present life, for example) but if she wishes to focus on her father you would be well-advised to agree to this and work together with her.

Third, there is the criterion of what will effect most change. To return to the example above, suppose that your client has been bulimic for seven years and to some extent it is currently 'manageable'. But she is annoyed with a work colleague and wants to make this clear to him. She wants to tell him to leave her alone. She is poised to do it. With your encouragement, if she goes ahead and states her feelings clearly to him, and he changes his behaviour, she will experience success. This may then form the first building block toward further changes. It will be a specific change and will offer a taste of success. Rather than making a vague attempt to alter the bulimia (which has been very persistent and will not change overnight) you can help your client with small, progressive, concrete changes first. The attitude required to be assertive in this case, for example, may initiate a further process of change that will ultimately help to overcome bulimia.

'You're pretty clear that there are these two or three problem areas. Which of these do you want to start with first?' This is a deliberate, closed-question way of eliciting a necessary agenda. You can, of course, explain why you think it is imperative to set clear priorities, but do this rather than wandering aimlessly through clients' anecdotal accounts with them. This is good practice in providing structure. Client priorities may alter during the course of counselling but by having agreed on what they are at the beginning you have helped the client into a disciplined process of counselling and personal learning. The starting concern does not have to be the most painful or obvious concern. It may be that the client wants to work first on something that will give her hope, that is easier or less anxiety-inducing. Mahrer (1989) asks clients to choose a feeling that is at the centre of their attention. He asks, 'Are you ready? Are you willing to start with this now?' At the heart of this is the importance of obtaining your clients' informed consent. What is crucial here is that you and she have agreed what you are working on together.

* Summary: Help your client to decide on priorities. Discuss the advantages of choosing to start with one in particular. Ensure that you are both committed to work on the same target concern.

---

24 Agree on a definition and conceptualisation of the target concern

---

You have an agreement on what your client's concerns are and what the priorities are. Now you need to go more deeply into the target concern (the issue you and your client have agreed to address). Let's look at an example:

Client: I just have problems relating to women.

You: Can you tell me a specific problem you have in relating to women?

Client: Well, when I like someone and I think she may like me, I still don't have the confidence to talk. Or I try but I dry up or come across as awkward.

You: So you'd like to be able to approach women you're attracted to and engage them in conversation. Are you saying that you can approach women or that you don't get that far?

Client: In the right kind of situation I can approach them, but then I get awkward.

You: So there are two possible problems here. One concerns the 'right kind of situation' and the other is your 'awkwardness' and how to overcome it. Is that right?

Client: Yes. I suppose I'm saying that I'm awkward around women and I don't want to be.

There are all sorts of possible directions to go in, but here the counsellor wants a mutually understood, focused definition of the problem. This is the 'what it is' and now we turn to the 'why it is', or how the client conceptualises it. How does this client understand his awkwardness in relation to women? Does he think he has a big nose? Does he think he may actually be gay? Does he think his mother made him anxious? Has he got the idea that everyone else finds it easy? Is he looking for some 'helpful hints for beginning Casanovas'? He may offer his own understanding of it or you may need to probe.

At this point it may help to explain your own view of such a problem. Explain that this is *one* way of looking at the problem but you are interested to learn if it makes sense to your client. Let's take an example of offering a conceptualisation to your client. It is from Windy's work with the client Steve (Dryden 1990: 47). I have already explained that what I'm going to say is only one way of looking at his problem but I have also said that I believe it may make sense to him. You don't want to put all your eggs in one basket by explaining that this is *the* way of understanding your client's problem. In what follows I explain the model of the role that irrational beliefs play in his problems. Note how I involve the client.

Windy: Right, so to recap, you're anxious about failing your Ph.D. Now we've agreed that it's not failing that makes you anxious but your attitude about it. Now it's important to distinguish between two types of attitude, one that will lead to anxiety and other self-defeating emotions, while the other will lead to concern and other constructive emotions. So if you bear with me, before we focus directly on your anxiety, I want to take you through an example that will help you to understand this important distinction. OK?

Steve: OK.

Windy: Now, I want you to imagine that you have £10 in your pocket and that your attitude is that you prefer to have a minimum of £11 at all times, but that it's not essential. How will you feel about having £10 while you want to have £11?

Steve: Concerned?

Windy: Right, or frustrated, but you wouldn't want to commit suicide. Right?

Steve: That's right.

Windy: Now this time imagine that your attitude is 'I absolutely must have a minimum of £11 at all times, I must, I must, I must', and you look in your pocket and discover that you only have £10. Now how will you feel?

Steve: Anxious.

Windy: Or depressed. Note that it's the same situation but a different attitude or belief. Now the third scenario. Again you have that same dogmatic belief 'I must have a minimum of £11 at all times, I must, I must, I must.' But now you look, in your pocket and you find that you've got £12. Now how will you feel?

Steve: Pleased.

Windy: That's right, or relieved. But with that same belief, 'I must have a minimum of £11 at all times', you would soon have a thought that will lead you to make yourself anxious again. What do you think that would be?

Steve: That I might lose £2?

Windy: Right, I might lose £2, or I might spend it or get robbed. Now the point of all this is that all humans, black or white, rich or poor, male or female, will make themselves emotionally disturbed if they don't get what they believe they must get. And they will also make themselves disturbed when they do, because of their demands, their musts. Because if they have what they think they must have, they could always lose it. But when humans stick to their non-dogmatic desires and don't escalate these into dogmatic musts they will constructively adjust when they don't get what they want or be able to take effective action to try to prevent something undesirable from happening in the future. Now I want you to keep in mind this distinction between non-dogmatic wants and dogmatic musts as we go back to your own situation. OK?

This is an example of a rational-emotive conceptualisation, but you will find ways of explaining concisely your own model so that the client knows how it works. Now, conceptualisation should be offered tentatively. On hearing your view of why a problem is a problem, and how it might be solved, the client may not automatically agree wholeheartedly. Suppose our client who feels awkward around women doesn't respond favourably to the £11 example, what do we do? This is the point at which you and he need to negotiate your conceptualisation of the problem. If he rigidly insists that his problem is because of his mother, and you rigidly insist that it is because of his dogmatic musts, then you will get nowhere. But if you both agree that some exploration of his relationship with his mother, coupled with looking hard at how he brings this into his potential relationships with all women, will be of maximum benefit, then you have a more mutual understanding of how you will work. To help you identify your clients' conceptualisations of their problems, we have included a questionnaire on clients' 'Opinions about psychological problems' (which was compiled by Chris Barker and colleagues) in Appendix 2.

* **Summary: Agree together on a definition of the problem to be worked on. Ask clients for their understanding of the problem and the factors that sustain it. Tell them your theory regarding the problem. Then negotiate a common way of looking at this problem.**

---

25 Specify goals related to the target concern

Once target concerns have been identified you need to help the client set specific goals for each of them. In brief counselling there is an overriding need for direction. This is not the same thing as counsellor directiveness, which tends to be based on the counsellor's frame of reference. Set goals collaboratively with the client that are specifically related to each target concern. We refer you to Sutton (1989) for a discussion on the importance of goalsetting. Sutton advocates specific written goals which are arrived at after some negotiation, which clarify mutual understanding and give clients concrete means of measuring their progress. Ryle (1990) incorporates this kind of ongoing monitoring of goals in his approach to brief therapy. Willer and Miller (1976) established fairly clearly that clients who were consulted in the setting of precise goals were significantly more satisfied with the outcome of therapy than those who were not consulted. Willer and Miller's research also found that a large percentage of clients were not consulted at all. Although this study was conducted in a psychiatric hospital setting some years ago, we believe there is still a strong tendency in many settings not to consult with clients, not to think of goals as important, or covertly to decide on clients' goals for them (e.g. 'this client thinks he wants to conquer his drinking problem but I know that he really needs to uncover a lot of deep pain').

The more specific goals are, the better. Although it is possible to work with a broad agenda of 'personal development' or 'straightening myself out', these agendas need to be broken down into concrete objectives. We are not saying this happens naturally or easily. It may take some time with certain clients to focus sufficiently to get a clear goal. But that is the direction we suggest you take. 'I just feel I'm not getting anywhere' is the kind of client statement that can mean many things. Goalsetting does not imply a facile 'So where would you like to get to?' response to such a client statement. Help the client to spell out what 'not getting anywhere' means, and what 'getting somewhere' would mean. What is really meaningful to the client here? Does the client need to talk about career development, making relationships, or about the possible origins of the 'getting nowhere' feeling, for example? Some approaches (e.g. reality therapy – Glasser 1984) home in sharply and quickly on what clients say they want and how their actions often contradict their desires. This style of rapid identification of goals and mobilisation towards attaining them is appropriate with some, but not with all clients.

'I don't want to have panic attacks every time I have to dine out, I want to be able to enjoy myself like everyone else' is a reasonably clear goal. The client has a strong motivation. Let's, however, look at variations on this theme. 'I never want to feel anxious ever again when I eat out or in any other public situation' is an unrealistic goal because of the 'never', and because the goal of total anxiety control is not in keeping with being human! Also, such a goal is not specific enough to work with. Avoid idealised goals. Learn to identify realistic, situational goals. 'I want to persuade my boyfriend that we don't have to eat out' is a goal which contains a wish to control another (the boyfriend) and indicates a wish for evasion. On both counts you will not want to go along with this kind of aim. 'I want to be able to explain to my boyfriend how stressful I find eating out' is an acceptable goal because it is honest and achievable, and points towards better coping. It is within your remit to help clients identify a goal the achievement of which is within their control. It is not, however, your job to talk your client round to your values. 'Yes, eating out is such a fuss, I think you're right to want to avoid it' is not something it is appropriate to say, even if you believe it, because for this client it is normative.

Let's look at how you help a client to operationalise a goal:

You: So your experience of panic recurs, it's acutely uncomfortable, and you want to be able to control or abolish it. Is that it?

Client: Well, I just wish it would go away, yes. But it's getting worse.

You: You wish it would go away, but it doesn't, and you've come to counselling to gain some insight into it and to find a way of overcoming it?

Client: That's right. I can't go on like this. Do you think I can
end it?

You: You're clearly keen to end it and I'm keen to help you. I
do have some ideas about how to proceed, but first I want to
be sure exactly what you want. You tell me you have a
dinner appointment next month and you'd like to be able to
'handle' it. Can you tell me what handling it would mean for
you? Are you willing to focus and work on that specifically,
for a start?

This shows the beginnings of work on a specific problem. Even
though the problem is clear enough, agreeing on a concrete goal
related to it is crucial. This does not mean that you can talk
about nothing else, but it does mean that you have a focal agreement. In this example the client's goal might be made more
specific by defining what is meant by panic and what degree (if
any) of anxiety is acceptable to the client in that situation and
what handling the anxiety means in specific terms. The client
may wander off the subject (and indeed may uncover material of
significance in doing so) and you too may be drawn into areas of
psychological interest that deviate from this goal. But if the goal
has been stated, it is at the very least a marker to which you can
refer. The ways in which your client wanders away from the goal
will also probably be very revealing. The example we're using
here may arouse doubts in the minds of psychodynamic counsellors: may not the anxiety related to eating out be a displacement
of some profound unconscious conflict? Of course, it may be.
And it may be that in the course of exploring the problem such
material will be uncovered. But it may not be. In the mean time
the client is distressed and clear about the goal of overcoming
that distress. Many counsellors set out to be too ambitious.
Remember Malan's (1975) findings that therapists are often prone
to 'over-determination' (wanting to trace every piece of the underlying dynamics) and to 'therapeutic perfectionism'. What is it
that the client has come to counselling for, at this time? Focus
on the goals that come from the client and take them seriously.
(A note of caution, however. Do not collude with pathological
goals, e.g. an anorectic client wishing to lose weight.)

Does the client have the necessary resources to reach her
specified goal within a reasonable time? Is it realistic, for example,
for our client who panics when eating out to expect to be able to
achieve results by next month? It may well be. Let's say she is
highly motivated, she's fed up with this disabling anxiety, she's

keen to get on with her life, doesn't want to mess things up, has support, and so on. But suppose she's had this problem for five years, she's getting very depressed about it, she's driven friends away instead of telling them about it, and she's been drinking a lot to try and forget it. The same goal may not be attainable in the same time. It may require longer-term counselling, and if so you need to help the client to accept this. But there could be other problems of personal resources. Let's say that she is not used to eating out, she's from a retiring, working-class family, has never learned to eat out, and to be assertive. It will take time for her to learn the skills she needs. She may lack the social skills that are taken for granted in the circles in which she finds herself. Don't make the mistake, then, of ignoring such variables.

Client temperament is an important area, often overlooked or not well understood by counsellors. If we take the subject of humour, for example, you might assume that it's normal and desirable for everyone to want to 'have a good laugh' as often as possible. That assumption can lead to the view that a client who is often very serious may have a pathological problem. This may lead to the prognosis that once the underlying pathology is identified and corrected, all will be well. But this overlooks individual differences and limitations. Do you assume that everyone has it within himself or herself to 'be anything you want to be', for instance? If change, challenge and perfectibility are important values for you, don't assume that they are for all your clients. Your temperament may be such that you strive for ever greater and greater 'self-expression' in the direction of extraversion; clearly, however, many people are contentedly introverted. In this respect, see van Deurzen-Smith's (1988) critique of counsellors' basic assumptions. Check that your goals and your clients' are aligned. Monitor any tendency in yourself or in your client to set up unattainable goals. Check, too, that your clients' stated goals are their own and not introjected ones. Elicit the client's aims and help them to distinguish these from your goals, the family's, the boss's, and those of others.

Depending on your approach to counselling, you may take a more formal or informal approach to making contracts for goal-setting. Stewart (1989) expresses a clear preference for formalised contracts. He suggests that when you make contracts you consider how feasible, how safe, how observable, how reinforcing of clients' autonomy, and how positively worded they are. 'I want to be able to go out to dinner and enjoy myself' is a positively worded goal, for example. If the counsellor and client agree to work specifically on the client's goal of enjoying himself in a specific situation, this is a formal contract: it may even be written down. You might consider the idea of 'hard' and 'soft' goals, too. 'I want to be able to relax and enjoy myself at that dinner' is a hard goal. 'I just want to know why I have these panic feelings' is a soft goal. Hard goals are specific and carry a high level of client motivation; soft goals are vaguer and often sound less convincing. (You may be able to see some connection between the specificity of goals and the stages of change at which clients present.) How hard, soft, formal and informal you are in relation to goalsetting also depends on your practice, your model and your personality. We suggest that the more you are able to vary your practice according to client needs, the better.

* **Summary: Set specific goals related to the client's target concerns. Collaborate in making these clear and workable. Check that they are really the client's goals, within the power of the client to achieve, and not idealised. Respect the modesty of clients' goals. Be prepared to influence clients where it is apparent that their goals are too difficult or too easy. Consider the merits of formal and informal approaches to goalsetting.**

26   Identify the client's past unsuccessful attempts at dealing with the concern

We pointed out earlier the importance of discovering whether clients had had previous counselling or other help and what benefits or otherwise they derived from such help. Here, we are looking at past unsuccessful attempts to change a specific problem. Although it is possible that clients arrive for counselling without having made any attempt to deal with the problem themselves, this is highly unlikely. The client may well have made several attempts to deal with the problem. So we encourage you to ask questions like 'What have you done in the past about this problem?' or 'What have you been doing to overcome this problem?' Such questions help the client to identify strategies that have not worked.

Let's take an example of someone who reports that he is 'stressed' and is worried about 'cracking up'. He says that his career has got out of control. In trying to extend himself, he has taken on too much work. At the same time he is earning too little. He has ensnared himself in a heavy workload and his plan to extend himself has gone wrong. He wants to know what he can do about it before something goes very wrong. You ask him how he has tried to deal with it (he has obviously not been successful) and he replies that he has refused pieces of work, he has talked to his partner about it, he has tried just to 'knuckle down to it' and he has meditated. None of this has worked, he says. 'Was it all hopeless or did some of those attempts work better than others?' you might ask. The point of your enquiry is to identify what has clearly not worked, and perhaps what holds some promise. You also want to avoid what's been tried before that has been unsuccessful, and to build upon past successes. Suppose he tells you that talking to his partner helped a bit, and meditating helped a bit. Find out how these helped, and how his other strategies didn't.

You don't want to offer to this client (or to any clients) a strategy that has already proved to be ineffective. If clients have never consulted a counsellor before, then this is something new for them, but don't assume that the novelty in itself is sufficiently motivating. The client may have a very supportive partner, but 'just talking about it' may not be enough. The client may be very good at being assertive, so don't unthinkingly suggest further assertiveness exercises. The question of what's been tried without success will yield important clues to how the client is likely to respond to your approach. Note that if the client were to say, 'I don't know what to try, nothing works', then a more global depression may be indicated, and if so, your task will then be to help the client identify specific target concerns.

Where a client appears to have tried several strategies energetically but without success, you may consider a more exploratory, unhurried approach, temporarily de-emphasising effort on his part. Where clients have apparently always become confused when discussing personal difficulties, you may consider new ways of helping them to be specific. Don't offer more of what has proved to be unsuccessful. Capitalise on what you are able to offer that differs from what the client has attempted to date. 'It seems to me you've been tying yourself in knots. How would it be if, when you come here, we focus on one thing at a time, and look at things in a relaxed way?' This may strike the client as sufficiently different from anything she's tried before to warrant hope. We are talking here about a client who has made strenuous attempts to change things. Clients will vary widely. At the other end of the scale you may be confronted by clients who have apparently made little effort to change anything, and there your strategy will be quite different again. You will probably have to help the client to *begin* accepting responsibility for himself. Note, however, that clients' unsuccessful attempts may include a lot of soul-searching or private thinking about a problem. Some people read magazines, listen to radio 'phone-ins', consult astrologers, do personal inventories of their strengths and weaknesses, and so on. Why have these not worked? What are you going to do that is significantly different?

* **Summary: Find out what your client has tried before that hasn't helped to overcome this particular problem. Identify which aspects of such attempts have been unsuccessful so that you can avoid further unsuccessful strategies.**

---

27 Identify the client's past successful attempts at dealing with the target concern

What we want to advocate here is that you aim positively to identify examples of where your client has had any success relating to a target concern. At first sight it may seem contradictory to speak of past successful attempts at problem solution, since if the problem is still there, then haven't previous attempts failed? It may be that some counsellors holding a depth-psychological view of change would argue that past attempts have been only symptomatic successes. Obviously within this brief focal view we are not taking this position. We concur with Prochaska and DiClemente (1984) that change is frequently cyclical (so many steps forward, so many back) and that it is important not to dismiss previous gains. We suggest that you avoid 'all or nothing' thinking in relation to your clients' progress (past and present).

Imagine that you have a new client who presents as very worried because after several months of abstinence she has taken a drink. She regards this as total backsliding and condemns herself for it. Now, of course there is a danger here of a serious relapse and you would want to address this accordingly. But will you join the client in her negative focus or instead concentrate on her clearly demonstrated power to be abstinent? This example illustrates that the same event can be viewed instructively or self-defeatingly. The potential here is for building on past success or for dramatising present 'failure'. (We are not dismissing the possibility here that a single drink might signal serious backsliding to come.)

Let's take another example. Your new client reports that she is very anxious about starting a new job after several years of being a full-time mother. You point out that she successfully held a number of jobs before becoming a mother and has successfully taken on the tasks involved in mothering and running a household. She has both past and recent successful experiences to draw on. She may be able to recall vividly the anxiety she felt on starting a new job in the past, or on first being responsible for a baby. Can she recall it and utilise it in her present concern? Clients often dismiss their own positive attributes and skills (e.g. 'I'm just a housewife') and you are advised to help them identify and acknowledge these positives when addressing present target concerns.

Referring back to Prochaska and DiClemente's stages of change, you may well have a client who has previously moved through the sequence of pre-contemplation, contemplation, action and maintenance. She has successfully conquered a problem. But now it reappears. Let's say a woman has previously overcome a self-defeating dependency on violent men. An old flame appears on the scene. She knows he is 'no good' for her but she is agitated, fearful that she will succumb to the old attraction. She is afraid of feeling powerless and helpless. How did she overcome this in the past? Wasn't the attraction just as powerful then? What were the factors leading to her ending the relationship? What were her personal resources? By focusing on how she handled change before, and maintained it successfully, you can reinforce her capacity to cope now. It may be that new strategies can be added to old ones, but by investigating old ones and harnessing them, you have a powerful ally.

You will also want to help the client to see precisely at what point she began to lose her resolution. What was different at this time in her life? How did she manage to stay clear of certain men for so long, but now finds herself all but succumbing again? Is it just chance? Is it that she's been unconsciously hankering to repeat bad experiences? Does she often encounter risk situations but usually handle them well? Are there other relevant factors in her life at this time, perhaps weakening her resolve? Look at both her past record of maintaining previous gains and the present threat and ask what the salient current features are. Help your client to put together her past successes and realistic potential for managing the future well. In introducing her to your proposed counselling approach, spell out those elements that will assist her in strengthening the coping skills she already has. Show her how you can help to minimise any tendencies to relapse further.

* **Summary: Explore with the client past experiences of dealing with the target concern. Investigate patterns of past maintenance and present threat to such maintenance. Build on past successes.**

---

28   Identify obstacles to change

It is important not to foster an overly simplistic view of change in counselling. Frequently, change is neither easy for the client nor predictable for the counsellor. While both commit them-selves to change attempts, there are various factors that may undermine their strategies. We therefore suggest that you make this clear and discuss explicitly any possible obstacles to progress. As with other material in this book, we are of course presuppos-ing that the client has a reasonably high level of honesty and awareness and that any unconscious factors are not so subversive as to wreck completely conscious change attempts. Put the question to your client squarely: 'What kinds of obstacles do you think there may be to your achieving this goal?' Be alert to clients who either want to please you by appearing 100 per cent com-mitted ('nothing's going to stop me') or who may be prey to naivety ('now that I'm in counselling there's nothing I can't achieve').

Having said this, look at what a client of Windy's outlined as her goals and her possible obstacles (see Table 1; reproduced with the client's permission). This is just one person's way of expressing her goals and possible obstacles. The obstacles here are expressed in terms of beliefs, fears and behaviours and are 'owned' as internal processes. The client is articulate and psychologically minded. Your client may be similarly oriented, but perhaps not. You don't have to get clients to write their goals and obstacles down. With some you may need to offer more examples than with other

Table 1 Goals and obstacles to change: one client's list

Ultimate goal: to get married and have children	
What I want to achieve	*What I think is stopping me*
To be able to form relationships with people – particularly men.	Inability to share my feelings. Inability to accept warmth/love offered to me. Fear of being 'owned'.
	Hypercritical approach to boyfriends which provides me with carte blanche reasons for not showing my feelings, accepting warmth, being 'owned' and forming close relationships.
	Fear of judgement towards my choice by outsiders: From parents – is he intellectual enough? From friends – is he nice-looking, a drip, etc.?
	Fear of being criticised.
Ability to share my feelings and allow myself to become close.	Shyness. Fear of giving away something of myself. Unaware of what feelings to share. Providing an opening through which others can get close to me and possibly entrap me. Total lack of practice – don't know how. Fear of my feelings being abused → rejection → hurt.
A real willingness to accept warmth offered to me.	Conscious rational thoughts: Is this Mr Right? Do I want to take from him? Do I want him to feel that I am his? Do I want him around a lot? Do I feel anything for him? Do I want to be seen with him? Do I want to share myself with him? Do I want to lose my independence?
	Feelings of insecurity in myself: Why does he want me?

Table 1 Continued

Ultimate goal: to get married and have children	
What I want to achieve	*What I think is stopping me*
	What is there in me to like? Does he want me or just the front cover? Is there anything behind the front cover?
	Fear of ultimate rejection → hurt.
To be able to express criticism openly (without causing pain), rather than bottling up grievances which allow me to abandon relationships or blurt them out aggressively.	Fear of hurting others. Fear of causing arguments and losing control of myself. Fear of rejection. Inability to find the right words.
Confidence when meeting new people or asking people to do things for me.	Shyness – diffidence. Fear of disdain.
Confidence when talking to people 'senior' to myself in some way, e.g. in school, inspectors, advisers, etc.; in politics, party bigwigs; in music, conductors, well-known musicians, brilliant players, etc. You.	Fear of being considered irrelevant or silly. Fear of being criticised. Fear of being disliked. Lack of confidence in my own worth.
The will to contact old friends who have left the area or I haven't seen for some time.	Belief that they don't really want to see me, talk to me, etc. Belief that I am an intrusion and disturbing them.

clients, perhaps by self-disclosing or by referring to others as examples. The task is to elicit connections between goals and internal obstacles, which represents the beginnings of insight. It also provides an agenda for active work on the target problems.

At this stage we are advocating that you help the client to identify general obstacles. The client may be aware that she is resisting progress. Or the client may attribute obstacles to the environment. 'I can't get on with people because they always snub me. Where I work, they're all hoity-toity, they don't want to know you', for example. Keep in mind the possibility that this client's psychological obstacles may include social skill limitations. 'Do you think there's anything at all you could do to improve the situation?' would be an appropriate probe. Or 'I can see that they might be difficult to get on with, but since you say you really do want to get on better, can you think of any ways in which *you* might do more to improve things?' might help to identify an inner obstacle. How might this dialogue proceed?:

Client: I don't know what I can do.

You: What have you tried?

Client: I tried talking to Deborah the other day but she didn't seem interested.

You: Can you tell me what you said to her and in what way you think she showed a lack of interest?

Client: Well, she just carried on typing as if what I'd said was boring.

You: She carried on typing. But how can you be sure what she was thinking? How do you know she thought you were boring?

Client: Well, why else would she ignore me like that?

You: There are several possible explanations of why she carried on typing, but you insist on your own version, with no proof. I think one obstacle is that perhaps you don't persevere with such conversations as much as you might. Another is that you're very ready to imagine evidence for people not being interested in you. Are you willing to accept that these *might* be obstacles in you, and not necessarily in others?

Client: I know what you mean, yes. Perhaps you've got a point.

With this kind of client you may have to be very persistent, returning to certain points again and again. But there are few people who are not willing to consider that their attitudes may play a part in what apparently 'just happens' to them. Show an interest in the client's world, including possible real, external obstacles. You are unlikely to insist with a black client or a woman, for example, that there are no social obstacles whatsoever to their self-advancement. Take the client's social context into account, their temperament, and so on. Get to know them; and in doing so, help them to identify blocks to progress and so to anticipate ways in which they might sabotage counselling. Transactional analysis has looked hard at client sabotage, particularly the kind in which a 'script' may be along the lines of 'don't succeed'. Stewart (1989) gives examples of how people create tragic outcomes for themselves and how counsellors can identify these and contract for a non-sabotaging outcome with the client. Clients have numerous ways of presenting obstacles, excuses, evasions, psychosomatic complaints, and so on. Don't run away with the idea that progress will be or has to be smooth – it is more likely to be an obstacle course – but go over the terrain with the client, mapping out what bumps and ravines you both think could stand in the way.

* **Summary: Invite the client to spell out possible obstacles to change. Allow for individual differences and accept the probability of set-backs, but bring the likelihood of obstacles explicitly into the picture. Accept the client's way of decribing goals and obstacles.**

---

29   Consider specific interventions for specific concerns

We are aware that many counsellors dislike the idea that there are 'treatments of choice' for certain complaints or problems. Common objections are that it is dehumanising to classify people or to pre-judge them clinically, and that people seeking counselling or psychotherapy should be regarded as whole people (not as isolated, 'medical model' physical complaints). Many counsellors, including those whose approach is psychodynamic and person-centred, claim that their approaches are equally successful with all kinds of clients. Mahrer (1989) regards experiential psychotherapy, for example, as potentially suitable for all (except those who, on trying it, decide it's not for them). Since a certain amount of research has suggested that there is little difference in outcomes from different treatment approaches, this has been taken by some to mean that anything can work with anyone. If this is your position, we suggest you consider, at least, the view that there are preferential treatment methods for certain problems.

Frances et al. (1985) reviewed research favouring both sides of the argument. On the one hand, there is ample evidence that relationship or 'non-specific' factors do contribute meaningfully to successful outcome in many cases. On the other hand, there is also ample evidence that certain problems are solved better by using specific interventions. Cognitive therapy works very well with depression. Behaviour therapy works better than psychoanalysis with alcoholism, smoking and eating disorders. Phobias are more appropriately treated by exposure to the feared object or event in real life than in imagination. The treatment of compulsions is more effective when some form of response prevention is included. Without consulting the research literature, or having a supervisor who does, you are unlikely to know these findings. Common sense often tells you when particular clients are not responsive to your approach to counselling. But an awareness of what others have found can greatly enhance your practice. In being able to conceptualise a client's problems when they call for specific treatment, you can either rapidly adjust your own interventions or refer on.

Striano (1988) interviewed people who had had unsatisfactory experiences in therapy. Many of these reported inappropriate treatments, including physical illness misdiagnosed as psychological, extreme therapist passivity or an over-analytical therapist style and the ill-advised uses of hypnosis and drugs. What this shows is that therapists of all persuasions are capable of error. It is not only the easy-to-condemn medical profession which errs. It is true that the talking treatments are less likely to be actually dangerous (except in cases where serious illness is overlooked) but you may be able to hasten a client's progress by identifying a specific concern and taking appropriate action.

How do you find out which specific interventions are indicated for certain problems? Obviously you will want to consult your supervisor, who also may or may not be familiar with certain conditions. Obviously you will learn to be discerning as you progress in your counselling career. In the short-term, however, the best way to find out is by consulting research literature. You might try, for example, *Clinical Psychology Review*, which contains excellent review articles on a range of topics relevant to counselling and psychotherapy. Garfield and Bergin's (1986) *Handbook of Psychotherapy and Behavior Change* is, in our opinion, an invaluable aid in familiarising yourself with research in the counselling field. Another source of precious information is the first-person reports of psychological disturbances written by people like Toates (1990) on obsessive-compulsive disorders, and Sutherland (1989) on 'severe mental breakdown'. Sutherland actually gives a consumer's-eye view of choice of treatment (pp. 258–62) which we as counsellors would do well to heed.

Please note that what we are not saying is that you must become a medically orientated counsellor. In line with the rest of the book we are arguing for putting clients first, even when that might demand extra work on our part or a willingness to re-learn or to refer clients on. If you are in doubt about any particular client, discuss this with your supervisor. Be flexible as to the way ahead. Be especially watchful in cases of prolonged non-improvement or worsening of conditions. As we noted earlier in Section 6 on referral, it is a good idea to become familiar with other allied professionals. When working in a mental health agency, Colin found a need from time to time to consult with other, external mental health professionals regarding particular clients. In some cases counselling was not the best choice for these clients, or needed to be complemented by appropriate medication. Indeed, the first time I ever met someone who had a serious obsessive-compulsive problem (in which he feared he might have been killing people) I did not at all recognise it for what it was. This client no doubt instinctively noted my lack of experience and dropped out of counselling. Now I am much more inclined to note and to act on signs of serious disturbance, rather than to assume that I can contain and aid such a condition in a purely person-centred manner.

* **Summary: Familiarise yourself with the research literature on specific problems and any indications as to treatment of choice. Be ready to adapt your approach or to make a referral. Always take any doubts to your supervisor.**

---

30   Explain the counselling approach you intend to use

Having obtained a good picture of your client and her goals, you now have a working hypothesis and a strategy in mind. You can now share with her what your intentions are. Together you have discussed conceptualisation of the problem and specific goals. While you may in general always be ready to invite the client to reflect on the counselling process, now you put to her your specific proposal. The approach you intend to take will be a distillation of various factors: your own counselling orientation; your knowledge of the client; your relationship with the client;

the client's previous history of the problem and attempts to overcome it; your knowledge of research as it applies (or not) to the client; and so on. You are ready to offer your understanding of the problem and your explanation of how you intend to help the client solve it.

Whether your preferred approach is person-centred, psychodynamic, cognitive-behavioural, transactional analysis, Gestalt, or whatever, you need to explain how it applies to your client's problem. You and the client need to have a shared understanding of how you are working. In Appendix 3 you will find the second part of the 'Opinions about Psychological Problems' questionnaire, devised by Chris Barker and colleagues. This questionnaire has forty-seven items covering possible explanations for how people may be helped to overcome their psychological problems. You may find it helpful to use this questionnaire to discover your clients' views of how they may be helped. You are likely to find it useful in pin-pointing the approach you use with each client. It can be done systematically, but you must judge the wisdom of that as you work with each client. Bearing in mind the degree to which clients differ, it may or may not be appropriate to use this kind of questionnaire systematically. But however you decide on your counselling approach, decide you must. So how do you put that decision to a client?

In each case the counsellor has to decide on an appropriate way of working with the client. It has been arrived at systematically, perhaps on the basis of the counsellor's experiences with similar clients, with reference to a supervisor, and so on. In each case the important thing is that you begin to explain, briefly, what you think is the core current problem and what you propose to do to deal with it. Each explanation contains a particular way forward which is expressed clearly, wihout jargon, and non-dogmatically. Depending on need, you might expand on your explanation. An obsessive client might ask for a detailed rationale. A client who is very informal might discourage you from offering too clinical an explanation.

Ask your client for her reaction to your proposal. Does it make sense? Does it fit with the client's perception? Is your suggested approach something the client feels able and ready to commit herself to? Is it focused enough? Would the client like to make any suggestions? Encourage your client to give honest feedback, and take seriously what she says, noting any non-verbal reservations she may signal. If she gives you a negative or equivocal response, probe for clarification and modify your

Table 2 Probationer blows a raspberry at apple therapy

Yorkshire's reputation for hard-headedness took a knock yesterday when a young probation defaulter told a court why he had failed to turn up for sessions of social therapy at a day centre.

The Crown court, where the realities of the world have traditionally been treated with respect, heard that the course required X to pretend that he was an apple.

Although a fledgling Olivier might enjoy this – nowadays, you could imitate an Apple computer or pretend to mis-hear and be one of West Yorkshire's many Methodist chapels – X was too thin-skinned.

The core of the problem, his counsel, Y, told the court, was that 'he couldn't understand what was being asked of him. He was embarrassed and stopped attending.'

Y explained that the apple was the fruit which broke the back of X, who is 19 and unemployed. He had not intended to blow a raspberry at the probation service, but had been baffled by the role played by the fruit in the curriculum.

'He had great difficulty in understanding some of the role-playing exercises he was asked to perform,' she said. 'He was asked to play various fruits, and the last time he went he was asked to pretend to be an apple.'

'I suppose there must be some meaning in these exercises, but he found it difficult to cope with them.'

X, of no fixed address, admitted breach of a two-year probation order imposed on him last December for burglary. He was ordered to do 140 hours' community service.

The probation service could not be contacted last night to give its answer to X's complaint – be it a lemon or otherwise.

(Adapted from the *Guardian*, 23 June 1987, with kind permission.)

approach as necessary. For a humorous illustration of the possible consequences of not explaining an approach to a client, see Table 2, which is reproduced from the *Guardian* (23 June 1987).

* **Summary: Be prepared to explain to your clients the approach to their problem that you propose to use. Explain this clearly, in concrete terms, and invitingly. Ask for feedback and accommodate this.**

31 Tailor your approach to the client

Remembering our earlier sections on client differences and counsellor influence, be ready to adapt your approach to the individual client. We advocate that you have a working alliance with your clients, that you do not use jargon and that you offer a specific approach to solving a problem.

Remember that clients have preferences for formality and informality, for expertness and attractiveness, and other counsellor styles. Now, when you are presenting your treatment proposal to a client who is a 'medical modeller' (or who expects psychological treatment from an authority figure – refer back to Section 21 on 'important client differences') and who looks up to you for learned advice, it would not be quite appropriate to give him a loosely worded description of his problems and of your proposed approach. In such a case a rather more 'professional' response might be called for. You might use slightly more professional language, refer to psychological literature and to your own experience of similar cases. If the client appears to want a didactic explanation, you might offer one (provided that it would enhance the client's progress rather than simply bolster your vanity). Conversely, a client who is an 'explorer' (again, see Section 21; see also Richert 1983) will not want authoritative diagnoses and prognoses, but an openness to experience. With him you will probably adapt your language, drop any suspiciously medical-sounding terms and employ colourful and 'experiential' descriptions. (Windy once had the experience, on misreading a client's cues and 'talking research' to her, of being told exactly what to do with his research!) In some cases you may decide to use self-disclosure (e.g. 'I had much the same problem myself and I found that what worked best of all was . . .').

Again, remember that these are not facile prescriptions but rough guides and ideas. When you are at this stage with a client and she is looking at you expectantly, and you are nervously wondering whether you've understood, your first attempt may not be quite the gem you'd hoped for. But goodwill, good practice and getting into the habit of the reflection process will all serve you well in maturing. Remember that the reflection process is a means of stepping back from the work and reviewing how well you and the client are relating, and how clear you both are about the agreed goals and tasks.

* Summary: In explaining to your client what approach you intend to take, bear in mind the importance of how you describe your approach. Ensure that you use appropriate language and that you invite the client's comments. Adapt your style according to the client's personality.

PART III
Initiating change

32   Begin work

'Begin work' may seem an odd phrase to use at this point, since you will have already done a lot of work with your client by now. Think of what has gone up to now as preparatory and inductive. Think of it as the laying of foundations. You might compare it to the large amount of work that goes into some buildings before any structure actually rises from the ground. If the planning, designing and foundation-laying aren't done, the building will collapse.

So you have decided with your client on target problems and specific goals related to them. You have talked about how you will be approaching the first problem. You have received feedback. Now you are ready to implement your plans. Be sure to proceed as discussed and do not succumb to sudden inspiration that will puzzle your client as to what is happening. (Inspiration has its place, but not here.) If you have agreed that you are going to give the client plenty of space to talk, and that you will mainly listen for some time, then do just that. If you have agreed to help your client to become more aware of his deeper feelings, then proceed to do that. If you have agreed to help the client examine thoroughly his dysfunctional beliefs, then systematically do that. Later there may be a place for some variation of techniques, but here be as methodical as you can. Patten and Walker (1990) discovered in a highly revealing piece of research that the people they interviewed (who had had marriage guidance counselling) *unanimously* found 'being given explanations about counselling techniques' helpful; 20 per cent found it 'very helpful'. In subsequent research (Walker and Patten 1990), when counsellors were asked for their views on explaining techniques, only 64 per cent considered this a helpful practice.

When you have covered some ground, enough to let the client get the feeling of your approach, ask for some feedback. 'How is this going for you?' or 'Is there anything you'd like to say at this point?' You are the best judge of when to ask for feedback. If your client is deeply involved in a needed cathartic experience, allow her the time or give her the support she needs. If your approach is person-centred, then close attention to the client's experiencing, including her experiencing of you, will mean that you stay closely in touch with her reactions, verbal and non-verbal. Where your approach is based on a sequence of taught steps, for example in some of the principles of transactional analysis or rational-emotive therapy, then you obviously have to allow sufficient time to do that teaching. But always check that you are explaining the approach clearly, and check that the client understands the approach and its usefulness to her concerns.

Suppose that you have had every reason to feel that your client is happy with the approach you have suggested. She has agreed that to look at her childhood, for example, may well lead to clues as to her present agitation. Yet when she begins to talk about memories, the activity of remembering seems remote from her current troubles. Perhaps she has difficulty recalling much, or remembers scenes but can see no connection between them and the present concerns. Invite this kind of information. It doesn't mean that you have to abandon your plans, but it suggests that some modification is called for. Some clients will be readily re-assured that a little time will reveal the efficacy of the approach.

Another danger might be that a client will feel rushed. If you are adopting a particularly confrontative or active approach, your client may well offer resistance. He may have liked the sound of what you had to offer in theory, but may find it very difficult in practice. Offer the client plenty of opportunity to give you feedback on any dramatic techniques you may use. Some brief therapies specifically seek to utilise the client's initial anxieties for thera-peutic movement (e.g. Sifneos 1972). Davanloo (1985) uses the first one or two sessions for a 'trial therapy' in which vigorous challenging of defences is coupled with the building of an 'un-conscious therapeutic alliance'. These highly active forms of psy-choanalytically derived technique are, however, specialised. The rapid entry into the client's irrational belief system as practised by Ellis (Yankura and Dryden 1990) is another example of an active-directive beginning to counselling. We suggest that as a beginner it is appropriate for you to pace yourself, to respect your own developmental needs and limitations as a counsellor as well as the needs of your clients. In general, then, heed the feedback of the client at this stage and be prepared to modify your approach.

* Summary: Begin your work with the client as planned. Watch for signs of difficulty or resistance. Ask for feedback on what you are doing and how it is received. Modify your approach if necessary.

33 Don't overload the client

We have pointed out in the introduction and need to reiterate here the importance of not bombarding the client with information, questions or demands. In the same way that you would not fire multiple questions at your client within the space of a few minutes, do not attempt to cover too much ground in one session. By all means offer more to clients who readily understand your interventions (for example, those clients who may have read about a particular approach or who have done similar work before) but be aware of what your client is really picking up. You need to be particularly alert to clients who may be afraid to question or confront you and we therefore suggest that you encourage all clients to let you know loudly and clearly if you are going too fast for them.

Remember to refer to the reflection process. 'We seem to have covered quite a bit of ground already. What's your reaction to this?' You might ask specifically, 'How do you feel about the pace we're going at?' Check out what the client has learned, because that's what important. 'Could you tell me what you've picked up from what we've just been talking about?' is a simple, direct way of checking. Don't assume that a lot of new ideas or a new way of relating to another person will readily be understood. Equally, don't worry clients to death with overly tentative questions when it's apparent that counselling is proceeding fairly well.

We think that one of the implications of being sensitive to individual clients' needs is a willingness to consider different session lengths. The fifty-minute hour is not sacrosanct, there's nothing of any intrinsic significance in it at all; it's just a convenience. Now, we are emphatically not saying that you should be undisciplined about timekeeping. Neither are we recommending that you change session lengths willy nilly. But consider that for some clients fifty minutes is a long time. Some people with debilitating physical conditions (like M.E.) find it very hard to concentrate or withstand emotional stress for very long. Some clients cannot benefit from long periods of self-examination and your feeling that you must fill out the hour may be taking them past the point of optimal learning. Lacan, for slightly different reasons, often terminated his therapy sessions after a very short time. Balint et al. (1972) refer to 'ten-minute psychotherapy', meaning the critical focus in each session which is experienced by both practitioner and client as a 'flash of understanding'.

The converse of this is being prepared to lengthen sessions. Mahrer (1989) and many other experiential practitioners allow ample time in each session for the experiencing and integration of strong feelings. In practice this usually means not longer than one and a half or two hours. This is explained to clients before the session begins. Other reasons for lengthening session time include crisis and practicality. Although as a general rule it is advisable not to slip over into extra time when your client appears distressed because this may convey the idea that distress (and particularly distress shown late in the session) will be rewarded. However, there may be times when extra time is quite valid. There are sometimes dramatic breakthroughs that may be better facilitated by allowing them to run their course rather than cutting them off. It may be that you are working with a particular client, helping her to break through some frozen emotion, and extra time, or the availability of extra time, may take the pressure off her. Practically, there are occasions when clients have to travel some distance to see you, or cannot see you for some weeks, and therefore request extra time in one or two sessions. Provided this is agreed, and suitable negotiations are made for extra fees, then there is no real reason not to consider this. (The obvious caveat is where you have a client who is trying to compromise you or to play games, in which case you will of course consult your supervisor.)

Another way in which you can help clients to maximise their learning is to tape-record sessions and offer copies of the tapes to them. This allows them to go over the session as often as they want to in order to ensure that its gains are internalised or that any doubts about the way you are working are aired. Try this and then ask your client to comment. 'Is there anything you weren't clear about, or anything you'd like to suggest?'

* Summary: Don't be over-ambitious within sessions. Listen out for what the client is actually taking in and learning and capitalise on that. Invite feedback on learning and on any problems arising. Be prepared for negotiating session length if appropriate.

34 Vary the level of support and direction

We refer you again to Howard et al. (1987) and the recommendation that you adapt your counselling style according to each client's needs. These authors suggest that two main kinds of counsellor style are supportive and directive. Supportive counselling involves relationship-building, empathy and acceptance. Some clients evidently 'thrive' in a climate of counsellor supportiveness, or the same client may at different times require either a predominantly supportive or directive style. A directive counsellor style is characterised by task-setting and goal-orientation. Although we have dwelt on goals to quite an extent in this book, we advocate an awareness of the needs for degrees of either style.

Remember that this is not a case of adhering to either one style or the other. Indeed, you will fare better if you are able to switch judiciously from one style to another as occasion demands. Let's say that your client has been working hard on a particular problem and has encountered a lot of pain along the way. You may have been very directive in helping him to get to this point. But then it is evident that he has reached a temporary plateau and needs time to digest his learning. You may at this time become much more supportive, perhaps suggesting to the client that he takes his time. You may perhaps acknowledge how much he has accomplished.

Howard et al. suggest that there are variations on this theme. You may, for example, offer a high level of direction *and* a high level of support at the same time, as in the activity of teaching. If you are using a counselling approach which is based partly on teaching (e.g. reality therapy), then you may support and direct simultaneously. Howard et al. suggest as an example of a low support/low direction therapist, the psychoanalyst who is an 'interested observer' offering neither obvious structure nor support. You will learn to adapt your level of support and direction according to each client's needs. To some extent these styles coincide with Heron's (1990) six categories of intervention, and it is worth familiarising yourself with Heron's model, which includes the prescriptive, informative, confronting, cathartic, catalytic and supportive interventions. The more you are able, in the early sessions, to respond flexibly to your client's shifting needs, the better the grounding you can provide for successful counselling. The more you practise 'changing gears', the better.

* Summary: Be aware of how supportive and directive you are at different times and consciously vary the use you make of these styles of counselling. Learn to adapt to the changing needs of clients throughout sessions.

---

35   Consider initiating between-session work

What we mean by between-session work is any assignment deliberately undertaken by your clients to enhance the impact of counselling. Your preferred approach may or may not include the idea of between-session work. We suggest that you consider its advantages in the light of what we said earlier about the importance of client activity in brief counselling. Your session is just one out of 168 hours in the client's week. All sorts of factors impinge on the client during the week. All kinds of opportunities for growth present themselves to the client in her everyday life. Budman and Gurman (1988) emphasise that 'being in the world is more important than being in therapy'. This is a point you may want to get across to clients who show signs of dependency on counselling or of reluctance to extend the gains of counselling into their everyday life. You will not be doing this if you do not believe in it – if, for example, you see the value of counselling as lying primarily in intensive transference cures. However, even psychodynamic counselling has its tasks for clients (Ursano et al. 1991) which include paying attention to dreams. Some psychodynamic counsellors instruct clients on the importance of recalling and if necessary writing down the contents of dreams.

Reinforce the importance of pyschological work in everyday life. This means that you may, for example, suggest to clients that they pay extra attention to their relationships, their moods, dreams, instances of avoidance, and so on. Stress from the beginning that counselling is one part of life or a temporary tool for better living, rather than a semi-permanent retreat from life's difficulties. Do this sensitively, according to clients' personalities and stages of change. With a client, for example, who is experiencing a hectic lifestyle, you do not want to add to that by setting a heavy schedule of homework. (In such a case you might begin to try out the idea that your client identifies a possible ten minutes in the day 'just for themselves'.)

We shall go into greater depth on the subject of homework later. The task for you to consider here is the argument for between-session work, your own attitude to it, and the timing and wording of it. It is easy to get into a pattern early in counselling that is hard to break later. Therefore, we suggest that you prepare your 'case' for between-session work. It might go something like this:

> It's clear that you're very committed to achieving your goals here. As you told me, you want to be able to walk into your office and not be overcome with anxiety about people looking at you and your getting the idea that you're inferior in some way. We can look at a lot of the problems here. But counselling works best when there's an active integration with everyday life. For example, if you were willing to begin to make notes of exactly how you feel and what you think when you walk into the office, that would help a lot. Gradually, I'd like you to be able to take a few risks with people at work, like asking them what they think about you. But for now, I'd just like you to bear in mind the power of practising new things between our meetings.

This kind of explanation paves the way. It gives an idea of what is to come. It helps to mobilise clients. Do it at an appropriately early stage, showing the relation between the client's initial goals and the achievement of a momentum in counselling. (It may be that if your approach is a person-centred or psychodynamic one, you will not want to be this directive at all; or you may prefer to use such ideas later in the process.) Adapt your explanation, making it as short or as 'authoritative' as will appeal best to the particular client. And of course refer the issue to the reflection process.

* **Summary: Since the typical counselling session is a small part of any client's week and the counselling process is a relatively small part of a client's life, think about tasks which can help clients consolidate their learning and extend it in the future.**

**36 Continue with the approach (or modify
as appropriate) until clients have
reached their goal or are confident of
reaching the goal on their own**

As you proceed with your approach to the client's problem, you
will inevitably notice her reactions. Whether your particular
approach is person-centred or more active-directive, the client
will have reactions to it from the very beginning. Although you
will have explained how and why you are working in the way
you are, your explanation may differ from the reality experienced
by the client. What we suggest is that you adhere to the approach
you have taken (and have agreed with the client), giving it a fair
chance to take effect, while at the same time observing your
client's reactions to it.

   Imagine that you and your client have agreed that it is important
for her to recall instances in which she has felt 'let down', for
example. She has agreed to scan her mind for memories and to
give details of when she has felt that friends have not supported
her. She has agreed that vague statements like 'people are always
letting me down' are not very helpful in locating the core of her
problem. So she sets out to identify specific instances of this
concern, and you give her plenty of time and gentle encouragement. But she gets frustrated. Perhaps she has consciously
complied with your suggestion, but less consciously she may be
feeling angry that you cannot instantly appreciate and agree with
her view of how people let her down. Because of this mismatch
between her reactive feelings and your attention to the chosen
approach, progress is awkward. You notice that she is restless,
sighs a lot, kicks at the carpet and claims that she can't remember much. What will you do in this case?

   In being persistent and being sensitive to your client's reactions,
you may well be confronted with a decision. In the extreme, you
might push for an outcome to your approach ('Come on, there are
obviously times you can remember when you've felt specifically
disappointed with friends') or abandon it altogether ('Well, this
doesn't seem to be working, so don't worry about it, forget it').
Avoid these extremes. You might elicit her reaction – 'I notice
how hard you're finding it to concentrate. Can you tell me what
you're actually thinking now?' If she were angry with you or the

'chore' of being specific, she may either then tell you so or deny it. Another avenue might be, 'If this isn't working too well, we can leave it for now and take a different approach.' Whichever way you decide to elicit her reactions, leave her with options. If you and she agree that the chosen approach is not working out, ask 'How do you think we need to change tack? Can you think of anything you or I need to be doing to help things forward?' This kind of question helps to consolidate the working alliance. When you notice signs that the client is withdrawing, or getting distracted or frustrated, do not ignore them or consign them to pathological categories. Even if there may be, for example, passive-aggressive features involved in the client not being able to re-member, respect her apparent difficulty. Refer to the reflection process (e.g. 'Perhaps the task of finding these specific memories is not quite right for you at the moment. I wonder whether you have another idea as to how we can get at this problem?'). This will reinforce your client's commitment to her targets in coming to counselling and it will reinforce your position as a flexible helper.

Sometimes clients don't give obvious signals that something is amiss. They may not be aware that there is, or they may be too polite or unassertive to say so. It is good practice actually to invite clients to raise any doubts they may have. Do this some-times even when there are no signs of doubt. This practice helps to create a climate of freedom and enquiry. It prevents the un-healthy accumulation of grievances and thus aids therapeutic momentum: when the client and you can quickly identify stra-tegies that are unhelpful and then discard or modify them, then energy can be devoted to problem-solving.

As you and your client continue to work, both of you may become aware of real progress. Let's say that your client begins to recall instances of being 'let down' by a friend and describes them in some detail. You then encourage her to distinguish be-tween her own interpretations of being let down, and other possible interpretations of events. She begins to realise with mixed emotions that she has indeed, in many cases, misinterpreted events. Gradually, with your persistent help, she comes to see that what has happened to her was perhaps not the awful trauma that she thought it was. Her mood may lift as she realises what part she has played in creating this recent cloud of 'depression'. You help her to prepare for her next meeting with her friend, and she can look forward to it with some relief and hope. Her first goal is in sight. When you and she are confident that this first piece of progress is consolidated, you can begin to reconsider whether that particular approach has any further use.

* Summary: Proceed with your chosen approach to this problem, giving it every chance to work. Be aware of your clients' reactions to it and invite their feedback. Raise any doubts clients may have about your approach and be prepared to change accordingly. Monitor the process until the particular goal is in sight.

---

37   Deal with any actual obstacles that emerge

Obstacles can emerge at any stage of counselling, and can take many forms. We have looked at the possibility of obstacles arising in the beginning stage of an approach to clients' problems. We have suggested that you be sensitive to signs that your approach is not quite appropriate or is not well received by your client. But there can also be obstacles in the way that you and your client communicate with each other. The hesitancies, doubts and instances of ambivalence that make themselves apparent non-verbally and paraverbally are important to look for. These are signs of possible 'ruptures to the therapeutic alliance'. Since it is important constantly to monitor the nature and strength of the therapeutic alliance and threats to it (Dryden 1989), we recommend that you focus on immediate experiences of such threats as appropriate. For example, when your client responds to one of your suggestions with faint enthusiasm and you see by her eye movements that her mind has wandered off, you might say directly, 'I sense that you're in two minds about what we're talking about here. Perhaps part of you is unconvinced by what I've said?'

Allowing for the complexity of human beings and therefore of the counselling process, you will understand that obstacles range from clients' defensive withdrawal or transference, to reasonable and conscious objections to particular interventions. Be alert to this complexity and avoid viewing every obstacle as necessarily either an unconscious conflict or a common-sense and pragmatic problem. To put this differently, both transference reactions and direct interpersonal problems in communication can and do occur in counselling. While you cannot guarantee always to eliminate transference, you can keep it in perspective by constantly encouraging clients to express their reservations overtly. In order to help clients do this with some comfort, indicate to them in various ways, from the beginning of counselling, that your 'ego' is not on the line. Let clients know that counsellors expect them to engage in interactions that are often more testing than normal social intercourse. Let clients know that their comments are welcome. Assure them that you take them seriously. Part of your job is to empower them and this is achieved by validating their struggle to articulate what feels 'right' and 'wrong' to them.

Now we need to modify these statements. Because transference reactions do occur, it is not appropriate to overlook them and to take everything at face value. Maintain a certain degree of scepticism. Watkins (1989) establishes how crucial it is not to overlook transference phenomena. Sometimes you notice certain refrains (e.g. the client may use a phrase like 'Well, *you* would know, wouldn't you?') which are directed at you but which clearly derive from another relationship or expectation in the client's life. Often these can be dealt with by responding, 'You often tell me that I know certain things which I may or may not know. You sound as if you know me very well. I wonder if I remind you of anyone?' Sometimes there is a fairly simple transference of identities of this kind and the client may readily realise and admit to the original identity. But often, too, the client may not be fully conscious of, or able to verbalise, how you remind her of someone important in her past, or how you evoke strong and significant feelings in her.

Casement (1985) is a leading exponent of the concept of unconscious supervision of the counsellor by the client. Casement advocates close attention to what clients say that may reflect something they feel about you. When clients do not feel understood or safe, for example, they may communicate this implicitly to their counsellor by using symbols from dreams or by talking about other people who have not understood them or kept them safe. It is a useful practice to listen for any such clues to clients' perceptions of obstacles. While some clients may say openly, 'You just don't understand me', others will let you know symbolically or obliquely. While we advocate that in brief counselling you do not want to encourage transference, you also cannot overlook it. Cultivate the art, then, of being aware of your clients' unconscious communications. Ryle (1990) considers that work with transference is a key part of his brief therapy model, as do all other psychodynamically-oriented therapists (Flegenheimer 1982). If you do work in this way, you may positively welcome the 'obstacle of transference' as an invitation into the client's inner world. By all means accept such an invitation, but within brief counselling you are advised to concentrate hard and to make overt any transference reactions as quickly as possible.

Sometimes an obstacle will be in the form of an obvious block. The client may stall every time a certain subject comes up. She may change the subject whenever you touch on something painful. When there is something of this sort, that is clear to you but not to the client, help her to disclose whatever is hidden or suppressed. Find ways of helping her to probe and explore. Feed back to her how difficult it appears to be for her to talk about her sex life, for example. Respect these difficulties but do not ignore them. At the very least make it known that you have noticed. If necessary agree to postpone exploration of such difficult subjects until later. But do voice your observations.

Returning to the more everyday obstacles, there may be something going on in the client's family, for example, that is a distraction for them. Perhaps they keep telling themselves that this is not the place to discuss it, but even so it is nagging at them and impeding progress in counselling. There may be something in the client's domestic or occupational life that has no obvious bearing on the problems they have brought to counselling, yet which preoccupies them. Or there may be worrying practical problems connected with counselling. Your client may be finding it very difficult to get time off work to come to counselling; she may be having difficulty paying for counselling. Such matters are not necessarily pathological, and sometimes there may be no short-term solutions for them, yet if they are not addressed they can seriously affect the quality of the counselling. Use your common sense and sensitivity in eliciting such concerns. It is not necessary or helpful in each and every session to search for possible obstacles to counselling, but you need to be attuned to signs of such problems arising.

* **Summary: Look out for any non-verbal signs that your clients are having difficulties with the way you interact with them; their transference reactions to you; painful or distracting issues; or practical problems. Encourage clients to voice *any* doubts or concerns.**

38 Be aware of, and respond to possible threats to the therapeutic alliance from, missed or cancelled appointments

It is possible at any stage of the counselling process to have the experience of a client simply not turning up for a session, without prior warning, or telephoning to cancel or postpone at short notice. Most counsellors will experience the frustration of waiting for clients who do not turn up for a first or second session. Obviously some people find themselves in crisis and able to make an appointment for counselling, but subsequently feel too anxious to follow through, or, having taken some action, either feel better or persuade themselves that they do not now need counselling. Too often, perhaps, the counsellor is unable to ascertain the reasons for clients not showing up for first or second or third sessions.

We address in Part VI on endings the subject of clients failing to turn up and how you may deal with this. But how should you respond in the earlier stages? We suggest that you write to clients who do not turn up, letting them know that they are welcome to make another appointment (if that is the case) and clarifying any implications for payment. Such letters are better kept brief and, although warm, to the point. Don't make people feel uncomfortable, but do be clear about what is and what is not on offer from you following a missed appointment. (You do, of course, need to be quite sure that you communicated unambiguously to your client the terms of your appointments in the first place.)

We think it is unlikely within the course of brief counselling that clients will choose to miss a session, and suddenly turn up to the subsequent session. We have known, for example, of clients in long-term psychoanalytic therapy choosing to miss an appointment (but having to pay for it) just to know what it feels like, or to test the therapist. But what does happen in brief counselling is that certain clients telephone to say they are ill; they may leave you a message or they may tell you directly. Sometimes they will say such things in a tone of voice that conveys ambivalence about continuing in counselling at all. Sometimes white lies are given because the client is not sufficiently assertive to tell you directly that she is disillusioned or afraid. Do not expect clients who are new to counselling to address you assertively and do not respond impatiently to people telephoning with 'excuses'. Politely state your readiness (or otherwise) to see them again at another time.

When clients cancel a session it can be viewed as a message to you. Whereas clients who disappear altogether before seeing you or after seeing you once may not be accessible for discussion, clients who miss or cancel but return need to be sensitively listened to for reasons and nuances. See Casement's (1985) method of learning from client's indirect messages to you. Some clients may know that actions speak louder than words, and their absence may be conveying something important to you. Perhaps it is 'Do you really want to see me?' or 'I'm not going to make this easy for you' or 'I don't know if I want to be here'. Absences can convey direct messages to you. They may also convey 'messages' from the client's unconscious about aspects of past abandonments, losses, and so on. Some clients come from chaotic family backgrounds in which unreliability is the 'norm', and they may repeat this behaviour with you. You don't have to be a psychodynamic counsellor to want to address the issue of a cancelled appointment, its possible meanings, and the threat it may pose for the therapeutic alliance (Dryden 1989). You do need to explore the idiosyncratic meanings of client absences, lack of punctuality and other signs of ambivalence or indiscipline.

Sherman and Anderson (1987) suggest several antidotes to the likelihood of clients' premature termination. Their review of literature on premature termination revealed, for example, that the sending of reminders after a missed appointment reduced first month drop-out rates from 51 per cent to 28 per cent. They also found that the use of 'imagination-explanation procedures' further helped to reduce drop-out rates. Such procedures may include having clients imagine themselves completing at least four counselling sessions successfully. You may experiment with this idea by simply asking clients about their general experiences of seeing through and completing tasks when they initially seem difficult. If you have reason to believe that clients may be wary of coming to several counselling sessions, or may need to have the 'culture' of counselling explained carefully to them, then it is worth considering such anticipatory exercises. Whether you anticipate the possibility of clients missing sessions, or you have to deal with it when it arises, consider what the client may be telling you non-verbally and how you can best respond in order to cement the therapeutic alliance.

* **Summary: Follow up by letter clients who drop out, but accept their decision. Consider possible reasons for missed or cancelled appointments, including cultural, idiosyncratic and psychodynamic factors. When the opportunity presents itself, address the issue appropriately.**

39   Begin work on a new target concern

Having helped the client to achieve her goal or to move substantially and predictably towards it, be prepared to move on to her next target concern. There is a temptation, perhaps, at this and later stages, to get sidetracked into client narrative that may not aid the change process. Help your client to recall the agreement between you as to prioritised concerns. Do not briskly move off from the first concern without checking that your client has, in fact, digested her learning and has achieved her goal or is in sight of doing so. But when you are sure that it is appropriate, address the next concern.

In raising the next concern, be sure that you do not assume that there is a connection between these concerns. There may be or there may appear to be, but ask the client about this. Let us suppose that an initial goal of standing up to her boss has been reached, and another goal is set which has to do with controlling overeating. Your client may consider that there is no connection between them, yet in learning that she has greater ability to withstand difficulties than she thought she had (in standing up to her boss) she realises that this improved sense of her abilities will also help her in addressing her overeating. In this case, you might proceed to work on the second concern using the same approach that you used on the first concern. The client, in this example, has understood how she can generalise her new learning from one concern to another. When you are faced with a client who is close to realising such a connection, you might say, 'I wonder if you can see any way of putting into practice what we talked about in relation to your boss with this concern with overeating.' You may be able to ease her into finding the connection.

However, progress is not always so smooth. She may successfully confront her boss, but see no connection between this achievement and her concern with overeating. Explain as well as you can any connection between these two concerns. Do so tentatively and ask your client for feedback. But if there are clear signs that your client perceives them as two quite separate matters, begin your negotiations on the second concern from a fresh perspective. Go back as far into the process of defining the problem as is necessary, letting the client talk and renegotiating an approach that makes sense to her. Show that you are open to understanding how she views this concern as separate from the first.

The process of moving from one target concern to another is a demanding one for the counsellor. Because you want to make the best use of of your time together, you realise the value of generalising learning from one problem to another. But because it is necessary to maintain a good working alliance, you will be constantly referring to the client's frame of reference. It is a fact of counselling practice that clients often experience confusion or distress as they confront stubborn personal problems. You may see clearly a connection between one concern and another and you may be impatient to demonstrate that connection. With some clients this will be easy to achieve but with many it will not. Help each of your clients to explore their new issues as fully as necessary.

* Summary: Be ready to move on to a new target concern. Where possible, help clients to generalise their learning from one concern to another, and take this process of generalisation as far as it will go. Where this is not immediately possible, help clients to trace the salient factors in their new concern.

---

40   Identify and work on themes rather than concerns

You can move from working at the level of isolated, concrete concerns by listening for themes. By themes we mean those basic assumptions, scripts or refrains that you become sensitive to as your work with a client proceeds. Themes straddle across the various concerns. There may be a connection between two concerns, but a theme is a 'higher level' understanding of what is involved. For example, your client may report that she feels criticised by her father, her husband and her best friend. She may not at first regard these as anything but separate instances of people causing her some discomfort. As you listen, you form the hypothesis that this client is very sensitive to criticism which may in fact be one of her themes.

You: Let me give you my reaction here. I wonder if, in a sense, the link here is a difficulty you have in coping with being criticised. We've talked about how your father, your husband and your best friend appear overly critical of you. Do you think you might be overly sensitive to criticism? If you do, we can look at what you're telling yourself at those times when you feel particularly criticised.

This kind of identification of a theme is offered to the client as a hypothesis. You put it clearly enough for the client to understand how you arrived at such a hypothesis, but you also leave the way open for disagreement or clarification. What you are doing here is bringing together elements from the client's story, and showing a possible linking theme. 'We've talked about situations *x*, *y* and *z*. Can you see a common connection here?' The client may, of course, reply that she cannot, in which case you will need either to rephrase your hypothesis or perhaps return to it later. Listen carefully for such themes and highlight them for the client. Even when she cannot see an immediate connection between concerns, she may well think over your hypothesis and gradually come to agree. As you work together, you have the opportunity to show her what theme is behind her many concerns: it may be, for example, that when she feels criticised she interprets this to mean that she is worthless.

In the example above, you might follow through with:

You: Let's see if, the next time you get upset, you can ask yourself, 'Am I getting upset at the criticism? If so, what am I telling myself in each case where it happens?' I'd like you to note these thoughts down and tell me about them next time we meet.

This statement effectively takes up a theme and shows how it can be observed and tested. The purpose of learning to identify connections in this way is to economise on time and to help the client to maximise her progress. The alternative procedure of taking each concern up as a discrete problem is time-consuming and risks some loss of momentum.

We have spoken here of a theme which neatly links concerns, but there can be several themes running through clients' concerns.

Don't assume there is only one, then, but listen for the two or three that may well be involved. Some approaches to counselling, like transactional analysis, 'specialise' in identifying scripts, mini-scripts, drivers, and other instances of important themes in clients' lives. In fact in TA it is thought that most people have one main driver and possibly one or two others. Stewart and Joines (1987) talk about the practice of 'driver detection', which is the art of listening for and observing signs of recurring themes. Even if you do not practise TA specifically, you will probably be aware of ways in which your client repeats certain patterns of behaviour and thought. In cognitive therapy (Blackburn and Davidson 1990) a major task for counsellors is to listen for clients' schemata, or ways in which they typically construe the world. Blackburn and Davidson advocate a process of helping the client to identify 'themes and words which recur' over the weeks of counselling. However you work, you will develop an awareness of how clients focus on and repeat certain themes.

* Summary: Listen for themes in what clients tell you, and raise these for discussion. Identify themes which link individual concerns, and help the client to understand how these predominate. Show clients how to focus on themes so that they can see how they operate in their everyday life and how they might work to change them.

PART IV

Encouraging change through homework

41 Explain your rationale for clients doing homework in general

We realise that some counsellors and counselling orientations are not in favour of employing homework assignments. The more relationship-based approaches are generally disinclined to introduce such between-session work. Macaskill (1985) differentiates between the 'being with' and the 'doing to' approaches, but shows that some psychodynamic practitioners (who are in the 'being with' group), including Wolberg (1980) and Ryle (1990), advocate the use of homework; and that Davanloo (1985) recognises the advantage gained by clients who work on problems between sessions. In client-centred therapy, Rice (1984) suggests that clients may be encouraged in certain cases to identify emotive situations between sessions as 'a very productive kind of "homework"'. In cognitive-behavioural therapy and counselling, homework is an integral part of the process. Blackburn and Davidson (1990) consider homework-setting one of the basic skills for cognitive therapists. Our own view is that the explicit use of homework assignments enhances therapeutic progress and should be thought of as basic skills for clients as well as counsellors.

What are the reasons for advocating that clients engage in between-session work? As we have pointed out previously, the typical counselling session is one hour out of 168 in the client's week. The course of counselling itself may consist of a few months in the client's life. Unless we are considering success in counselling to result mainly from fortuitous factors (e.g. the 'non-specific' relationship factors) we are forced to ask how the process of change actually occurs. Research into brief psychotherapy (see Koss and Butcher 1986) suggests that a variety of factors contribute to successful outcomes, and clients' levels of activity rank among these. By learning to implement new behaviour themselves, clients reinforce their commitment to change. The interaction between the counselling session and the everyday world is important in confirming for clients that they are the agents of change and that they have the power to change. This interaction can be made explicit, and we believe it is wise to make it so in brief counselling. Unless clients are told about the benefits of putting what is learned in counselling into ongoing practice, there is a risk that they will learn by default to be rather passive in effecting change in their lives.

Explain to your clients, then, that it is usually helpful to engage in some activity related to counselling between one session and another. You do not have to call this activity homework. 'Homework' to many people conjures up an unpleasant image of difficult and undesirable schoolwork. You may decide to try other terms, like 'assignment', 'task', 'practice' or 'between-session work'. Indeed, for some clients with a preference for activity, *any* such ideas may be welcomed. But you may also describe the nature and desirability of homework without using specific terms. 'Perhaps you can consider what it might be helpful to do between now and our next meeting in order to focus better on your concerns' is the kind of statement which invites clients to take up homework without actually calling it by that name. You might illustrate the purpose of therapeutic homework by referring, for example, to learning to play the piano: the lesson is important, but practice during the week is essential. Homework does not have to be obviously 'behavioural': any activity relating to counselling and change can be useful, including thinking about what to discuss, making lists of items to discuss, and putting aside time in the week to reflect on counselling issues. Encourage clients to view themselves as active investigators of their cognitive processes, feelings, behaviour and psyches, in the counselling-room and in their living-rooms and offices.

In cognitive-analytic therapy, homework 'represents the enlistment of the patient as her own co-therapist and serves to promote self-awareness and self-control and to minimise regression' (Ryle 1990: 30). If you and your client are committed, together, to a goal-directed approach to counselling, there is likely to be little difficulty in communicating your rationale for homework. If you have reservations about homework, you are likely to communicate them to your client. We suggest that you acquaint yourself with the arguments for homework being an integral part of the counselling process, before you discuss the subject with your clients. When you do discuss it, notice your client's non-verbal reactions and invite her to put these into words. Deal with any reservations and correct any possible misunderstandings in a respectful manner.

* Summary: Consider your own views on homework and what evidence there is for or against it. Explain its usefulness to your clients in whatever terms are most acceptable to them. Convey the idea that homework accelerates progress and helps clients to become their own counsellors. Invite feedback.

42   Think broadly about different types of assignments

As we have said, homework can cover many different tasks. We give you a sample here: reading, writing, questionnaires, monitoring, behavioural tasks and imagery.

Reading

You may wish to ask your client to read some specific text relating to the kind of counselling you practise. Models which rely on teaching certain schemata, like transactional analysis and rational-emotive therapy, are often well-explained by relevant literature. When clients agree to do such reading, they are helping to accelerate the counselling process, they are saving session-time, and they are becoming an active participant in change. Some counsellors (e.g. Scott 1989) give specific reading material to clients with certain problems. Scott uses, for example, a short 'handout' called 'There's Hope' with people who are depressed. Often such short texts are very useful with people who have specific addictive problems. Some counsellors advocate large 'doses' of reading, which constitutes a kind of bibliotherapy in itself. You would do well to discriminate between clients who may and may not benefit from such reading assignments. People who are illiterate or who are already overloaded with other reading commitments (e.g. students) may not take kindly to the idea. Also, aim to match the level of reading assignment to what the client will feel comfortable with; otherwise you may risk demoralising the client.

Writing

It is often useful to ask clients to write something about themselves. This can be done in various ways. The simplest is a brief, first-person account of salient material. 'What I want from counselling' is one way of constructing such an exercise. In some settings, clients are asked to complete full 'life stories' for presentation within a session. Personal construct counsellors (Fransella and Dalton 1990) often ask clients to write a self-characterisation, which is a short description as if from the point of view of someone who knows the client as well as anybody could possibly know her. This exercise, and many others, are used in cognitive-analytic therapy (CAT). In CAT, clients are engaged in many writing assignments, including letters addressed to the counsellor. (Ryle 1983 suggests that writing assignments fit well into a psychodynamic framework.) It is sometimes helpful to ask clients to write a letter to a father or mother, or anyone who is significant to them. Such letters need not be sent, since the very writing of them can be cathartic or instructive.

Questionnaires

We have referred earlier to the questionnaires of Chris Barker and colleagues which can be used to elicit clients' views on counselling (Appendices 2 and 3). There are, of course, many questionnaires designed to elicit psychological information. Common examples are the Beck Depression Inventory, used in cognitive therapy; the Psychotherapy File, used in cognitive-analytic therapy; the Structural Profile of multi-modal therapy. All these questionnaires elicit information directly from the client and provide the basis for focused work in sessions. Needless to say, some people (counsellors as well as clients) dislike questionnaires, so you need to be sensitive to their use, and explain their rationale carefully.

Monitoring

It is a good idea, and one commonly practised by cognitive-behavioural counsellors, to ask clients to spend some time between sessions looking at their own behaviour and noting, in particular, times of stress or difficulty and accompanying thoughts and reactions. This exercise can be done by simply keeping a diary. It can also be done formally by completing, for example, a 'daily record of dysfunctional thoughts' or a 'weekly activity schedule' (see Blackburn and Davidson 1990). Structured exercises of this kind can be particularly helpful for clients who are depressed and who have difficulty focusing on specific situations.

Behavioural tasks

You may care to suggest simple behavioural tasks or more systematic behavioural strategies. Asking your client to get up earlier in the morning, to spend more time looking for a job or to spend ten minutes each day tidying his room, for example, are all tasks which may help a client incrementally towards greater self-efficacy and coping. You may teach your client assertiveness techniques, such as rehearsing clear statements, saying 'no' without qualifying it, and so on. Or you may, at an appropriate time, suggest to your client, for example, that he takes the risk of asking out a woman, asks for a raise at work or tells his brother that he loves him. Self-control desensitisation and flooding are examples of formal be-havioural exercises (see Bellack and Hersen 1987).

Imagery

Some clients are particularly responsive to the use of imagery. You might teach a client relaxation exercises, for example, which incorporate the use of visualisation: 'You are walking through your favourite peaceful setting, it is a beautiful day, warm and bright, and your worries have evaporated, you can forget them.' Clients who readily engage in such imagery can often use similar imagery in their own everyday lives. This process can be enhanced by making a tape-recording of your instructions and offering it to the client. Imagery can also be used, of course, by asking your client to draw or paint images of special significance, and to bring them to a session for exploration. Imagery often helps clients to express feelings which are hard to verbalise.

This is not an exhaustive list, but it is intended to remind you of what is available and to stimulate you into considering creat-ing your own exercises. Since each of your clients is unique and has a different learning orientation, different homework assign-ments will be appropriate in each case. Ask yourself questions like: Could a particular piece of homework jog this client out of his impasse? Is it time now to get this client to take some risks in her life? What is the best way to help this client get in touch with these difficult feelings between sessions? Is there a way of overcoming the amount of stress my client experiences in certain situations? How can I construct appropriately helpful tasks for my client? Such questions are ones that you may well want to take to supervision.

* **Summary: Familiarise yourself with the variety of homework assignments it is possible to use. Consider what uses your clients can make of various kinds of homework. Ask yourself how well you can integrate particular kinds of homework into your own approach in a way that will best help your clients.**

---

43   Allow adequate time for negotiating homework in the session

---

When you are first introducing the idea of homework, you need
to allow sufficient time to do this. You also need to introduce it
sensitively, not being so anxious to 'get it in' that you cut into
something important that your client is already working on. Once
the idea of homework is established and genuinely agreed by
your client as acceptable and helpful, it is good practice to get
into a habit of setting time aside for negotiating homework. We
suggest that you allow five minutes at the very least, before the
end of the session, to talk about and set up a homework assignment. If you do not do this, your client may feel rushed, you may
convey the feeling that homework is not an integral part of counselling and that your client is not, after all, an equal partner in
homework negotiations. Anticipate, then, the need for time at
the end of the session. If you should find yourself without sufficient time to discuss homework, it is probably better to omit it
altogether rather than to rush it.

It is sometimes the case that an obvious or likely assignment
is suggested by something the client is discussing in the middle
of the session. If so, note this and return to it at the end of the
session in order to formalise it. Whether it is the case that you
get an idea or the client comes up with one half-way through the
session, don't be tempted to dwell on it there and then, because
it may well be superseded by other material and then get forgotten.
Your client may say, for example, 'I know I want to say something to her, but I'm not sure how to put it.' Noting this, you
might suggest, 'That seems like a worthwhile idea to follow-up.
Shall we discuss at the end exactly how you might prepare to say
what you want to say to her?' You are both then free to continue
with other work, and you have a useful item for homework.

Interestingly, Albert Ellis, pioneer of rational-emotive therapy,
which places a high premium on homework assignments, con-
fesses to not always remembering explicitly to set or check it
(Yankura and Dryden 1990: x). While he regularly suggests to his
clients that they read one of his books and listen to audio-cassettes
on RET, he says, 'I sometimes neglect to check up on clients'
specific agreed-upon homework . . . because I get too absorbed in
some of the things they are telling themselves and in disputing
their irrational beliefs. My forgetfulness in this respect is my

problem – perhaps stemming from my own low frustration toler-ance'. This is a reminder that we will not always get things right in our counselling, but it is a good idea usually to prepare our-selves for negotiating homework.

* Summary: Leave sufficient time to negotiate homework. Allow at the very least five minutes at the end of the session. Don't be tempted casually to set homework in the middle of a session. Be sensitive to your client's need for time.

---

44   Explain your rationale for specific homework assignments

---

While you may have given a broad outline of the usefulness of homework, when it comes to specific applications you need to think again. Clients may readily agree with you that homework 'sounds like a good idea' in principle. Such agreement may be too readily offered, for example, by compliant clients. The concrete task of discussing homework and preparing to carry it out, how-ever, is a test of commitment and understanding.

Suppose that you are at the end of the second session with a new client. He has been telling you that he gets very 'wound up' at work when people put pressure on him. His goal is to 'feel relaxed' and 'not to get defensive' in these situations. Together you and he have started looking closely at what he is telling himself about such daily events and his reactions to them. Now you suggest to him that he notes his thoughts and reactions at work. You ask him to write down the thoughts he has before, during and after an occasion at work when people 'put pressure' on him. You might explain that we frequently misinterpret events according to our previous learning experiences; we often expect things to go wrong, for example, even when they are going well. Suggest to him, in this example, that people may or may not actually be putting pressure on him. Ask him to monitor carefully any similar event, along with his thoughts, to check on how he construes 'pressure' and how he makes himself tense and de-fensive. Suggest that he writes his observations down. Tell him that by establishing the links between events at work, his own thoughts and feelings at the time, and his being 'wound up', he may be able to discover the root of this particular problem in himself, and resolve it.

* Summary: Carefully explain to your clients your reasons for suggesting a particular piece of homework. Show clients the thinking behind it and show them how it relates to their goal in counselling.

---

45   Negotiate, don't set

There may be an assignment for your client that appears to you as if it will be obviously necessary or clearly helpful, but your client may not at all agree with you, or may appear to agree but silently resent your assumption that you know what is right. There is certainly nothing wrong in your having good ideas about homework assignments, but always check with clients whether they regard them as appropriate ideas. Some clients are especially sensitive to authority issues, and if they sense that you are beginning to impose ideas on them, they will be likely to react adversely. Since the ethos of counselling is built around respect for clients' autonomy, it would be counterproductive to ignore your client's autonomy.

Describe the assignment you consider suitable for your client. But then invite his reaction. At the same time, watch for his non-verbal responses. If he half-heartedly agrees with your idea, put to him your observation that he doesn't seem very enthusiastic. Encourage him to voice his doubts. Ask him if there is any way he would like to modify the assignment, and be genuinely keen to meet his ideas. If he still seems equivocal about it, ask 'Can you think of anything you could do between now and next week which would be more helpful to you?' Allow him to construct his own assignment. Reinforce the proposition that homework helps clients to change, but de-emphasise any idea that you are 'in charge' of it. Stress that it is a collaborative endeavour.

There is a subtle danger that in avoiding the setting of homework, and placing emphasis on negotiation, you may be tempted to abandon or seriously dilute the idea of homework. Your client, for example, may be a better negotiator than you are, and a better game-player! Indeed if there is any struggle going on between you and your client, then it may surface in the issue of homework. If this is the case, refer to the reflection process. Ask your client how, in view of his reservations, he feels about homework and the way you discuss it. If such a discussion becomes an obstacle, consider the possible transference issues involved. Macaskill (1985) and other psychodynamic practitioners are fairly confident that homework negotiations will raise transference issues, which should then become an appropriate focus for work. But another perspective on this is that the more you place responsibility with the client, the fewer such problems between you are likely to arise. By encouraging your client to suggest his own homework, for example, you show him respect. 'How might you put what we've discussed into practice between now and next week?' is one way of negotiating rather than setting homework.

* **Summary: Don't present homework in the form of an order. Respect the client's autonomy and invite comments on your ideas. Modify assignments or allow the client to suggest alternative assignments. Focus on obstacles which may arise at this stage.**

---

46   Ensure that homework arises out of the session's focus

You may well be tempted, in reflecting on what your client has told you, to think of an 'ideal' piece of homework which you can suggest to them at the next session. Or you may hear of a particular exercise and wish to put it into effect. We suggest that you do not do this. Rather, note the idea but save it for an appropriate occasion.

It is advisable that any homework assignments relate to what has been discussed in the particular session. This means that you are called on to be creative. This is why we advocate that you familiarise yourself with the range of possible homework assignments so that you can adapt as necessary to each client at each stage of their counselling. Spend the time in sessions listening to your clients, and allow assignments to formulate themselves in your mind without distracting from the discussion in hand. An assignment will be much more powerful if it follows naturally from the material that has been discussed in the session. It should act as a bridge between the session, the client's target concern, and the goal at any particular stage of counselling.

In the early stages of counselling you will probably not want to suggest challenging homework tasks that risk scaring clients off. You will allow clients time to understand the approach being used, and time to unravel the elements of their concern. The homework used, then, should reflect the client's stage of learning. Sensitively judge assignments to match the client's ability to carry them out. But also match them with the immediate concern. If your client is aiming to overcome a social anxiety problem, for example, and you are in the early stages of counselling, it may be appropriate for her to monitor her thoughts, and recall scenes from her past when she felt such anxiety. If, in a particular session, she talks about a certain place she used to visit which she associates with 'funny feelings', you might suggest that she writes down her thoughts and memories about this place. This would provide a link between the 'there and then' and the 'here and now' and between her in-session concerns and her target concern. This would fit in with her wish to understand why she feels anxious in certain situations. At a later stage, you might suggest to her that she deliberately puts herself in certain situations in order to confront the anxiety. But at an early stage, such a task could well be quite inappropriate.

* Summary: Link a homework assignment to what is discussed in the session, suspending any temptation to try interesting but inappropriate exercises. Be mindful of the stage of counselling your client is at, and link homework with target concerns appropriate to this stage.

> ### 47   Agree to the content of the task, being mindful of the client's abilities, circumstances, learning style and past history of doing homework

---

When you come to formulating the precise piece of homework with your clients, it is important to take into account their ability to perform it. You may have in mind a very promising idea for homework which, however, simply may not match what the client can do. Writing tasks are an example. Writing may come very easily to you but perhaps not to your client. (Or it may come easily to most clients but not to some.) At the extreme, your client may be illiterate or may have certain difficulties with writing. The client may or may not have told you and may be willing or not to let you know. If you have reason for doubt about this, elicit such information sensitively and if necessary find another way that your client can do the homework assignment. You also need to take any disabilities into account. Again, some disabilities may be obvious but others not. If your client has trouble concentrating or thinking systematically, then don't set any complicated thought-monitoring exercises, for example. Don't ask clients to perform any exercises requiring mobility that is beyond their ability. A subtle example of this is M.E., a debilitating condition which often makes sustained physical or emotional effort very difficult. When it is apparent that there are such obstacles, look for other ways of presenting assignments.

Another kind of possible obstacle is sometimes found in the client's circumstances. Consider, for example, the issue of your client's personal finances. She may have discussed this subject with you or it may not have come up at all. Suppose that you discuss together your client's wish to meet more men, and you suggest that one way to do this is through the small ads in certain magazines. Some clients will readily agree that this is an appropriate and practical course of action to take. But it does cost money. It is possible that your client is paying you whatever disposable income she has, she may have other commitments, or she may be receiving state benefits. Don't, then, assume that what is possible for you is equally possible for your client. (We suggest, too, that you don't assume, as some therapists do, that 'if you want it badly enough, you can always find a way to afford it'; some clients do live on very limited incomes and may not have the skills required cleverly to juggle finances.) Consider your client's home or living environment and how this may impinge on her ability to carry out tasks. You might suggest that she meditates, without realising that she lives in a crowded and noisy flat, for example. (She may be able to modify this after practising assertive skills, but there may still be difficulties.) You might suggest that your client listens to a tape of your session together, without realising that the only tape-recorder she has access to is in a unit standing in a shared living space. You may tell your client how important it is that she goes out, joins classes, and has fun, without realising that she lives in a small village, has no car and experiences severe practical difficulties in getting to places.

In addition, take into account your client's values. It might seem relatively easy for you to confront your father, for example, but it may be very hard for clients from particular cultures to question the authority of their fathers. Your client may have sincere religious, political or other affiliations which preclude certain kinds of behaviour. Of course, these may need to be questioned as part of counselling, but don't assume that all such positions are pathological or secondary to, say, white middle-class therapeutic values.

Consider, and ask about, your client's learning style. Is she someone who learns best from reading and reflecting, or rather from direct action and risk-taking? Is she more likely to respond to an assignment using imagery? Will she respond better to highly structured work or to homework which leaves her room for her own creativity? This information may become apparent from counselling sessions, but you may have to make it explicit by asking, 'How do you best learn?' Give her some examples of learning experiences. Ask her how she has learned best in the past. Which learning experiences has she found most exciting, enjoyable or challenging? Which experiences has she found most unrewarding or frightening?

An important principle to bear in mind is what Windy (Dryden 1991) has called 'challenging but not overwhelming'. When you are constructing appropriate homework, remember to pitch it at a level which maximises motivation and learning without paralysing the client with fear. Describe your ideas for an assignment and then negotiate an appropriate level of risk or effort. It is important to involve the client fully in the fine-tuning of setting the task. The task has to be not only sufficiently unlike the client's everyday routine to involve new learning, but also sufficiently palatable and performable to avoid the client sabotaging it. Look for non-verbal reactions to your suggestions. Suppose that your client expresses a fear of driving, even after having passed her driving test. You suggest that she takes a drive around the block next Tuesday; she looks unmoved. You suggest that she drives up the M1 in the rush-hour; she looks terrified. Perhaps she will be more responsive to the idea of driving to a place on a Sunday afternoon, where she will be greeted by friends who will give her dinner. Find the appropriately motivating task by talking it over with your client. Remember that clients have expectations regarding tasks. Efficacy expectations are expressed in the forms: 'Can I do it? Do I have the capability for this task?' Outcome expectations are expressed in the questions: 'Will it help? Will this task help to lead me to my goal?'

Finally, consider the client's history of doing homework. She may have done assignments with you before, or with another counsellor or helper. If not, she will probably have executed homework tasks at school or college, or perhaps as part of a job. The usefulness of discovering such past attempts lies in the clues they may give to her attitude to different tasks and the manner in which they are set. By taking into account the above factors, you are more likely to be successful in arriving at suitable tasks for each occasion.

* Summary: When presenting your idea of what kind of task will be helpful, consider whether the clients will be able to do it; whether clients' environment and resources will permit them to do it; whether their learning style matches the kind of task suggested; whether the task represents challenge rather than being overwhelming; whether their past experiences of homework are relevant.

---

48   Check that the client understands the assignment and its purposes

Clients may agree to your propositions regarding homework without fully understanding them. There is a lot for clients to think over in most counselling sessions, and sometimes they are still turning over information in their minds from earlier in the session when you are discussing an assignment. So keep this in mind. The chances are that if you work through the stages of explaining and negotiating homework, then you and your client will be tuned in to each other at this point. But do check that this is the case. Does your client understand why you are suggesting this piece of work? Does he truly understand it, or is he merely nodding an empty assent?

A practice that is recommended is the writing down of assignments. It has been found in the field of health psychology that written reminders of behaviour to be practised are very important in enhancing change attempts. Some counsellors use purpose-designed stationery for such written records of assignments. You can get, for example, a no-carbon-required pad which will record for both you and the client the assignment agreed on. (You can even get joke prescription pads on which you write your psychological prescriptions for clients. This can add a dose of helpful humour to the proceedings.) Omer (1990), in discussing the concept of 'promoting expectancy', suggests that announcements in appropriately expectant tones of voice can help to reinforce messages of importance. 'Now I am going to give you your homework for the coming week', he suggests as a useful formal announcement, for example. Against this approach, we would argue that it minimises the client's input into the homework setting. Don't underestimate the importance of the part your client has to play in discussing and designing homework.

* Summary: Allow for the possibility that your clients may not immediately understand what you are asking them to do, and why. Consider reinforcing homework messages by committing them to paper and underlining their importance.

49 Agree when and where

Again, although the client may appear to have understood and approved the assignment, she may still leave the session without a clear idea of exactly how she will carry it out. It might seem like 'a good idea at the time' (during the session) but in the cold light of day, at home, without support, it may lose some of its clarity.

It helps to concretise the assignment if you talk about when and where it is to be carried out. 'When do you think you might be able to do this?' may elicit some clear commitment. But the client may respond with, 'Oh, sometime in the week, I suppose, when I have the time.' This is clearly a vague, ambivalent response. 'It's often helpful to consider a specific time' is a possible rejoinder. Similarly, 'Where do you think would be a good place to do it?' will encourage the client to picture herself in an appropriate situation. Gently move your client into as specific an agreement as possible. Negotiate with her any obstacles to choice of time and place. If she does live in a noisy flat, for example, ask her where else she might go to carry out the assignment. By going through it in this way, you reinforce the importance of homework, helping the client to visualise herself doing it and putting it firmly into time and place. This makes it far less easy to forget or sabotage.

* **Summary: Negotiate and agree on the best time and place for your client to carry out the homework assignment.**

---

50   Distinguish between 'try' and 'do'

Stewart (1989) gives several examples of how clients protect themselves from real commitment to change. A primary device for avoiding commitment is that which is worded as 'I'll try'. When you ask your client if he is ready to go ahead and complete a particular assignment, and he tells you that he will try, it is a good idea to pick him up on it. 'I'll try to do it' is such a commonplace phrase that it is easy to accept it at face value, yet if you look at what it means it becomes apparent that it represents an escape clause. When you ask someone, 'Will you do this?' the most direct replies are 'Yes, I will' or 'No, I won't'. When someone replies, 'I'll try to do it', this frequently means 'I'm not really committed to this idea and I doubt if I'll do it'. It can contain the nuance, 'I may do it but if I fail to, then I can always say that I only said I would try.'

Listen for this, or similar ambivalent phrases. (Stewart suggests that 'I want to', 'I can do it', and 'I think I will' are comparable.) If you sense that your client is speaking ambivalently, confront this. 'You've said you'll try, but will you?' is an obvious counter; or 'I didn't ask you if you would try, but if you will do it – will you?' Because 'trying' smacks of halfheartedness, it is advisable to elicit commitment. If you allow the client to 'try', then you may well be giving them the message that you do not regard their efforts seriously. Confronting people with this issue need not be accusatory. Delivered in a straightforward, even humorous, way, it conveys your concern for the client's progress. It sometimes helps to demonstrate to the client what the difference between trying and doing is. A simple and vivid example is to ask the client to 'try' to click his fingers without actually clicking them. Then ask him to 'do' it. As he immediately clicks his fingers he can vividly appreciate the difference between trying and doing.

Stewart advises, too, that you listen for even more subtly hidden ambivalence. A client may say 'I will do it' in a tone of voice or with accompanying bodily gestures that say, 'But don't be surprised if I don't do it'. So be alert to non-verbal reservations and share your perceptions with the client. 'Are you sure you will? You sound a little hesitant to me' might be your response to such ambivalence. Elicit your client's commitment, but avoid being persecutory!

* **Summary: Do not allow your client to leave you with an 'I'll try' response. Point out the ambivalence in this phrase and seek your client's commitment to carrying out the assignment being discussed.**

---

51   Identify potential obstacles to homework completion

The ambivalence towards homework embodied in the phrase 'I'll try' is just one example of the obstacles that can arise in relation to homework. We suggest that you actively help the client to identify any present or embryonic obstacles to completing assignments.

Ask your client if she is aware of any factors in herself, in others or in the environment that may stop her from carrying out her homework. She may be aware of some resistance, for example, as you are discussing the assignment. Some clients may say, 'I realise that as we're talking, I'm actually thinking that there's no way I'm going to do this homework' or 'I'm catching myself planning how I'm going to tell you next week that I was too busy to do it'. Not all clients will so readily disclose such thoughts, however. You may need to probe a little. If the assignment involves others, then how will your client use these other people as an excuse for not completing her assignment? If there are environmental constraints, these need to be discussed before the session ends so that alternative assignments free of such constraints can be discussed or steps to overcome the environmental obstacles can be taken by the client. Here as elsewhere collaborate with your client in finding realistic ways to reduce or eliminate all such obstacles.

You may notice various signs of resistance to homework as you talk with the client. Perhaps she quickly changes the subject, or looks blank, or sullen. Perhaps she has told you how often she gets into battles with 'authority figures' in her life. 'Do you think that might crop up here?' is a question that might help her to confront a potential pattern of sabotage. Such questions can be put in a lighthearted manner without losing their importance. What you are trying to do at this stage is to minimise self-defeating obstacles and maximise commitment.

* **Summary: Ask your clients what possible obstacles exist between them and the successful completion of homework assignments. Explore such potential barriers to progress as fully as necessary.**

---

52   Initiate mental rehearsal

Clients are often helped to prepare for homework assignments, particularly those which involve some degree of risk, or behavioural challenge, by engaging in mental rehearsal. You will often hear people retorting, 'Oh, I just couldn't see myself ever doing that!' You can demonstrate to them that they probably can see themselves doing it, even if the image is accompanied by apprehension.

Mahrer (1988) put forward the idea that an ideal experiential therapy session consisted of four steps, the last being the rehearsal of 'new ways of behaving in prospective scenes'. The client pictures and experiences herself acting as she would like to, and this mental rehearsal is aided by having her eyes closed. For example, she may say that she cannot picture herself asking a man out. So you guide her through a brief visualisation of just such an occurrence. She may become self-conscious and laugh. Ask her what is happening; ask her to continue with the picture: at what point does she begin to find it difficult? Help her to follow through the rehearsal as far as possible, identifying along the way any snags, and then imagining ways to overcome them.

Encouraging your client to anticipate and rehearse such scenes reinforces the efficacy of homework. She can see that it is indeed possible that this task will achieve something important for her. Note that you are not conveying any guarantee that what she envisages will 'come true'. What you are reinforcing is the idea that the steps leading up to such risk-taking are within her control. You are also encouraging her to foresee obstacles and to engage in problem-solving in relation to them.

* Summary: Have your clients picture themselves carrying out the homework assignment, including any problems which arise along the way. Use the mental rehearsal to reinforce the client's power to carry out the task and to problem-solve.

---

53   Establish criteria for success

It is advisable to establish with the client how she will know that the homework has succeeded. What will constitute success? Take the example of the woman preparing to ask out a man. She has never done it before and always considered it as being beyond her range of possible behaviours. Now she can see that it is possible for her to do it. Nothing can stop her from asking a man out. But at what point will she have succeeded? If she interprets the assignment as asking a man out and having him accept the invitation, she may well be disappointed, because she cannot predict or control his response: he may well say 'no'. In this case, seek her agreement that success lies in her bringing herself to ask him out, and nothing more. If he accepts, this is a bonus, but if he declines, she has still succeeded in completing her assignment.

Assignments which involve other people may prove particularly problematic. In these cases you need to establish clearly that the criterion for success lies within what the client can achieve for herself. If she has always wanted to sing in public, and does so, this is success, even if she does not get the applause she would like, because that is outside her control. The environment and other people are outside her control. Ensure that she understands this and that she truly accepts that when she has discharged her task, she has succeeded – whatever may follow.

A predictable problem for some clients is the projection of

perfect success. In the example of the public singer, she may wish to sing 'perfectly', or like another singer. Your task then is to help her to accept a realistic baseline for measuring her performance. This may be that if she finishes the song, success is hers. It may be that if she sings in tune she will have succeeded. These tasks are probably within her control. 'To bring the house down', however, is not a realistic goal. With clients who are perfectionistic you need to spell out the terms of success with special care: it is the doing of the assignment, not brilliant execution, which is success. You may even have your perfectionistic client deliberately perform in a mediocre fashion, in order for her to learn, for example, that she can accept herself when she does less than perfectly.

* **Summary: Ensure that your clients will be able to measure whether they have succeeded in carrying out their assignment. It should be within their personal control and should not involve perfect performance.**

---

54   Explain the 'no-lose' nature of homework assignments

While you will strive to set meaningful and testing pieces of homework, you also need to remember the non-judgemental nature of counselling. You do not want to create a new set of 'conditions of worth' for your client, so that she will feel good if she succeeds and bad if she fails. The objective of homework is to accelerate and consolidate learning, but not at the risk of inadvertently reinforcing your client's sense of failure.

Accordingly, explain to clients the following three possible outcomes from homework:

1 They will do it well, and as a consequence will probably feel good, and all will be well.
2 They will do it badly, and as a consequence may feel bad. In this case the opportunity presents itself for them to give and get feedback on what happened.
3 They will not do it at all, and as a consequence will, again, have the opportunity to give and receive feedback on how and why they did not do it.

Whatever the result of the nature of the assignment, something will be learned. This is what we mean by a 'no-lose' assignment. In describing this idea to your clients, they will likely feel considerable relief. We do not suggest, however, that you present the no-lose explanation in such a way as to commend the poor-performance and non-performance options. Convey the desirability of success but avoid conveying any insistence on it. Paradoxically, many people perform better knowing that they do not have to do well. In particular, anxious clients may benefit from hearing this no-lose clause.

* **Summary: Let your clients know that no matter what outcome there is to their homework assignment, something will be gained.**

---

55   Check homework

Having carefully negotiated a homework assignment, if you fail to follow through and you ignore the subject the next time you meet, you convey the idea that homework is not important after all. Even more damagingly, you may undermine the client's respect for you and for the counselling process. So, if homework is worth setting, it is worth checking.

At the beginning of the session following an agreed assignment, say to your client, 'Let's first of all talk about what you and I agreed that you would do. Tell me how it went.' This is a straightforward invitation to discuss the outcome (whatever it is) of the homework. Do not be afraid to enquire. Your client will be expecting you to ask. Your enquiry does not have to be persecutory, in the sense of 'checking up on' him. It is, rather, respectful of his efforts.

It is usually a good practice to begin the session with this enquiry, but there may be instances in which your client arrives in distress. In such cases you will naturally allow appropriate space for ventilation of distress. But don't let this throw you off the subject of homework. Return to discuss and check the homework before the end of the session. Use common sense in regard to this: obviously if your client has undergone a major unforeseen catastrophe, do not pursue the subject of homework. On the other hand, be alert to the possibility that some clients may wish to divert your attention from the agreement regarding homework.

* **Summary: Do not overlook homework. Check on what progress clients have made with their assignment. Initiate open discussion of what was learned from it. Be sensitive to the timing of your enquiry.**

---

56 Check whether or not the client did the homework successfully

First, check what the client learned from the experience. Take, again, our client who was to ask a man out. She returns and tells you, 'Yes, I did it, and he said he'd love to go out with me. I was amazed!' She learned that to ask assertively for what she would like actually paid off – she got it. Alternatively, she might say, 'Yes, I asked him out and he was quite pleasant but said he already has a relationship.' What did she learn? Perhaps that she had the ability and courage to do something new and risky, that she didn't feel as anxious as she thought she would feel, she felt, in fact, only mildly awkward when he told her he was already in a relationship.

Did the client learn what was intended (that she was capable of asking a man out and that regardless of the response from him she could come out of the assignment with self-respect), or something else? It is quite possible that there will be an unexpected outcome. Suppose she asked the man out, he said he would like to go out with her, and she realised that she was not so interested in him afer all. This may lead you to a further chain of enquiry. Or suppose that he said he would like to go out with her and he had been trying to summon the courage to ask her out; she might learn from this something about the universality of social anxiety, or about how much time can be wasted by such anxiety. This client might, on succeeding in this assignment, suddenly realise that she had spent her whole life putting things off; or, more mundanely, she may learn that this man really isn't her type.

When you respond to the client's account of success, avoid giving approval to her as a person. Rather than saying, 'You did really well, you're fantastic', for example, try something more like, 'That was really good'. This latter statement praises the deed, not the client. It introduces or reinforces the idea that actions are more or less desirable, but people are not to be rated on the basis of their performances.

* Summary: Discover what the client learned from doing the homework, whether the learning was that intended or not. Capitalise on this progress, but direct your enthusiasm at the accomplishment rather than the person.

---

57 Check whether the client attempted the homework but did not succeed; discover the reasons for this

If the client says that she failed to do the homework, explore what she means. Ascertain whether or not the client actually began to do the homework. An attempt is different from an 'I'll try' in that the former is a wholehearted approach to doing it (which fails somewhere along the line) while the latter has an element of ambivalence about it from the very beginning. When it is apparent that she did make a serious effort, praise that effort (e.g. 'it was good that you started to do it') rather than the client.

Find out what happened. Ask for the details. How far did she get with the assignment? What ran through her mind as she approached it? Was she aware of a specific point at which she realised she wouldn't follow through to the end? Was there, after all, something in the environment, or not within her control, which prevented her from succeeding? To return to our client who was about to ask a man out: she may report that she got as far as talking to him but lost her nerve when it came to proposing a date. Her effort can be applauded and something can be learned from the precise factors which prevented further success which you need to discover. She may say that she went out to a place where she knew she would meet someone she liked, but panicked and returned home: this could present quite a different picture of her level of functioning; by pursuing this further, you might learn, for example, that she panics in other situations too, and this may indicate that you need to adjust your approach with her. It could be that she got as far as asking him out, but sabotaged it subtly by asking in a rather negative way. Be encouraging about the degree of success achieved, no matter how small, and use the details to discover what the problems are and how they might be resolved.

Remind the client that the assignment was a no-lose one. Tell her that it is helpful that her attempt has yielded useful information on which to proceed to work. Then consider the way forward. Depending on the circumstances, you might suggest that she simply repeats the assignment again next week. Or you may suggest some modifications to it. What you can also do is to show how this partial success has within it certain links with her other obstacles to change, thus reinforcing the importance of the homework. It also gives important clues to what you need to work on together with the client in terms of the nature of the block. It is really acceptable to fail, but advisable to persevere in order to effect long-term change.

* Summary: Find out how the assignment did not succeed, including the details. Praise the client's effort, and not the client personally. Elicit from the details factors which can serve as data for problem-solving.

---

58 Discover reasons for the client not attempting the homework

Dryden (1990) shows many of the reasons for clients not attempting their assignments after they have been set (see Appendix 4). These include misunderstandings over the nature of the task; 'excuses'; rationalisations for not doing homework in general; objections to the stress or difficulty involved in the task; forgetfulness; depression; reassessing the assignment as inappropriate. You may well give clients such a list to prompt a discussion about how they blocked themselves from doing the homework assignment if they really don't know why they didn't do it.

Again, elicit the details of the client's thinking in relation to the homework, and identify the obstacle so that you can work to overcome it with the client. At what point did she decide not to do it? How did she convince herself not to do it? How does

she feel about not doing it? How does she feel abut the counsellor having set it? Was it truly negotiated, rather than set? Emphasise again that within a no-lose arrangement, it is good that
this information can come to light and lead to further discoveries.
Refusal to complete the homework might represent the client's
hatred of having things imposed on her, for example; she may
have realised that she didn't want to do it, but she was too afraid
to tell the counsellor, and therefore showed her feelings indirectly,
by not doing it. This discovery can lead to new insights and
directions in counselling. Consider ways to design new or modified
assignments.

*** Summary: Find out why your client did not attempt the
homework and work with the client to explore the obstacle.
Discover possible reasons by initiating discussion on the client's
feelings and attitudes regarding homework. Renegotiate or modify
the assignment in the light of what you and your client have
discussed.**

---

59   Encourage the client to take increasing responsibility in setting homework assignments

---

Having negotiated homework assignments with your clients, you
have given them a taste for discovering what homework works
best for them and how to design it. Clients will learn some of the
skill of designing suitable assignments from you. Their commitment to homework will hopefully grow as they discover the impact
it can make on their learning. But it may not automatically follow
that the client takes over the responsibility for setting assignments
from you.

Since you have shown your clients how you design and negotiate
homework, they may realise that they can do this for themselves.
The value of doing homework may be clear to them, but you
may need to make a direct suggestion. 'How would you like to
think of an assignment for yourself this week?' might be a simple
way of putting this. Or, suppose that the client is facing a particularly momentous challenge in her life; you might suggest
that she considers what piece of homework will be sufficiently

potent to help her face this challenge. Let's say that she has to address a large audience and is feeling very anxious; you might ask her to construct an assignment that will help her to desensitise herself – she might, for example, force herself to speak up in front of a meeting of senior managers at her office, or to rehearse her speech in an empty theatre. You may give her ideas, but gradually withdraw your initiative and encourage hers.

If she claims not to have the imagination to think of assignments, for example, you might ask her, in a given case, what sort of assignment she imagines you might set her. Alternatively, you can encourage her to brainstorm: 'What are all the possible ways you might rehearse this forthcoming speech? Just list them without too much thought, however bizarre they are.' Ask her to write them down. Having listed various realistic and unrealistic possibilities, she can then proceed to look at the pros and cons of each one, and to choose one which is suitable and efficacious. Using humour and imagination can stimulate a sense of learning by fun. Alongside the fun, however, you need to convey the message that the goal of brief counselling is to help your client towards autonomy: therefore, the more she takes responsibility for devising and executing homework assignments, the better the prospects for her future. Again, as with other matters, this needs to be communicated non-judgementally and with a readiness to explore obstacles.

* **Summary: Gradually encourage your clients to take over the setting of homework assignments. Help them to do this by demonstrating how it is done. If appropriate, initiate a climate of humorous exploration of possibilities. Reinforce the rationale for autonomous task-setting.**

---

60 Set homework assignments for yourself in order to empathise with and help the client more effectively

In general, counsellors are advised to have some experience of being in counselling, in part to learn what it is like to be a client. We advise you, too, to experience homework assignments yourself. First, by setting yourself homework assignments you will appreciate the technical issues involved. Second, you will experience some of the thoughts and feelings that clients experience in undertaking homework. Third, you will be able more authentically to negotiate and follow through on homework assignments with your clients if you have undertaken similar assignments yourself. Fourth, you may also come to appreciate the problems and benefits involved in self-generated homework and self-change generally. Finally, you can set yourself homework directly related to your counselling with particular clients (e.g. consulting relevant research literature or devising a form to elicit certain information).

How do you go about all this? If you are still in counselling you can ask your counsellor for help with homework assignments. However, if you are not in counselling, you can still effectively undertake homework. What current or chronic obstacles or discomforts are there in your life? You may be relatively free of crises, but most people always have areas in their lives which can benefit from attention and change. Do you, for example, procrastinate, avoid certain situations or people, chronically underrate your abilities, or experience mild anxiety or depression? If so, use your own insights and learning to focus on specific concerns and to arrive at goals that can be operationalised. Then use the same procedure we have outlined in the previous sections to set appropriate assignments for yourself; adjust your ideas as necessary to find a good fit between your focal concern and the precise assignment.

It can be an instructive exercise to do homework in parallel with your client. Take, for example, a problem which is about as difficult for you as the client's is for him, and try to mirror his efforts in real concerns in your own life. This kind of exercise keeps you in touch with what clients are facing and helps you to remain inventive. In some cases it can be useful to self-disclose to clients the kinds of difficulties, successes and failures you encounter. We refer you to Section 42 on different kinds of homework for suggestions on what you might undertake yourself.

* **Summary: There are various benefits of doing homework assignments yourself. By setting assignments for yourself not only will you achieve personal learning, but also you will strengthen the bond between you and your client.**

PART V

Counselling in the middle phase

61   Follow through on themes and consolidate gains

It is not possible to state exactly when the middle phase begins, since the length of counselling relationships, even in brief focal work, varies. Clearly, however, there are certain characteristics of a beginning phase, as there are of the ending phase. The middle phase tends to be a time of deepening trust and intimacy between counsellor and client; a working pattern has been established. At the same time, difficulties may arise: impasses between client and counsellor may appear; and the client may get into deeper material.

Keep your client's focal concerns in mind. When you are well established in the counselling process, a good deal will have been learned. Build on this by gradually introducing your client to wider applications of what she has learned. We have already discussed the idea of identifying themes (by which we mean scripts or overarching dysfunctional beliefs and attitudes) rather than individual concerns (or problem areas in clients' lives). By the time you are working in the middle phase of a counselling relationship you will probably have many opportunities to work thematically. By this we mean that you can, increasingly, draw out themes from the examples of everyday concerns that clients give you, and work more intensively on these. Remember not to treat each session as if it is the beginning session: capitalise on what you have both learned and move forward.

If your client has reported several instances of fearing the disapproval of others, for example, you may work on how her thinking contributes towards those fears. Perhaps she gradually learns in counselling, and by homework assignments, that she can have an argument with someone and discover for herself that she does not have the dire need for approval that she thought she had. Extend this thematic learning by helping her to look at other situations in her life where she imagines that she has a great need for approval. What you are then doing is to provide your client with a method, a philosophy or technique for dealing directly with her life and its future problems. This is where, although the counselling may be brief, you have the chance to practise 'seeding' for future client changes. Seeding is the act of offering and reinforcing change goals which may not be realised until some time after counselling ends (see Zeig 1990).

You may have held firmly and successfully to your original approach with the client, but at this stage you are still in a position to extend the learning that is possible from that approach. Dryden (1990) demonstrates how the counselling process in rational-emotive therapy adapts according to the stage of counselling. But as well as adapting your approach from stage to stage, and from each of your client's concerns, you may come to realise that certain aspects of your approach work better with particular clients. Remaining within an RET approach, for example, it may become apparent that your client responds consistently to rational-emotive imagery, rather than to strictly verbal and logical examinations of her thoughts. In other approaches, it may emerge that your client has an obvious preference for linking insights in her life now with events from her past. She may respond very favourably when you try an exercise based on psychodramatic techniques. By the middle phase you may well identify a particular modality (e.g. imagery or behaviour, among others) which suits your client best (see Lazarus 1981). If this is the case, capitalise on this by reinforcing lessons learned through this modality and by introducing any further exercises belonging within it.

* **Summary: Continue work on your clients' focal concern and gradually help them to extend what they have learned from specific situations to more general applications. Work thematically and identify any particular modality in which your client learns better.**

---

62 Keep on track with respect to original concerns

The other side of generalising from specific concerns to thematic learning is that original concerns may be forgotten or put aside prematurely. There is a danger that your client will wander from one subject to another rather superficially. (This danger is one that the critics of brief counselling often level against counsellors: that by encouraging 'superficial' problem-solving and 'flight into health' you encourage the client to gloss over deeper, more painful and subtle, well-defended material.) Return to the original concern as often as seems necessary to ensure that your client is not running away from it and is not 'problem-hopping' or 'solution-shopping'. In other words, while brief counsellors deliberately practise selective attention, they do not advocate avoidance.

Do not allow your client to lure you into casual conversation, or into long discussions of red herrings. You need to be as alert to the defensive or symbolic use of conversational decoys as any psychoanalyst, and we suggest you draw your clients' attention in such instances to what they are doing. Ask them if they are aware of how they are changing tack in the conversation. Ask them if they are anxious. This is easier to detect when they are obviously going off at a tangent from the therapeutic task at hand. A subtler form of escape from threatening inner anxieties is often shown through compliance. The client may welcome your demonstration, for example, of how to generalise from one concern to another and how to work thematically. He may be only too keen to get away from certain raw bad feelings associated with his presenting problem. You need to be on the lookout, therefore, for any such manouevres.

* **Summary: Keep the original concern in mind and return to it until you are both sure that it has been fully addressed; do not be drawn away from it for defensive reasons.**

---

63 Balance the gains of being goal-directed against the gains of relationship factors

We have stressed throughout this book the need to maintain a central focus or foci. Relationship-building is often seen as a primary concern in the beginning phase of counselling. However, it may be that you will risk what Rowan (1989) calls 'aim-attachment' (that is, being overly concerned to produce results), thus minimising the power of relationship factors in the middle phase. Clarkson (1990) draws attention to the importance of 'the multiplicity of psychotherapeutic relationships'. These include the 'I–You'; 'the working alliance'; 'the transferential relationship';

'the developmentally needed relationship'; and 'the transpersonal relationship'. We have alluded previously to the working alliance and to transference factors. Reference has been made to Buber's (1947) emphasis on the significance of two human beings (I and thou) meeting at a particular time. A central plank in our argument for brief counselling has been the use of the reflection process, which is based on respect for the client and for the need for mutual understanding. We have also discussed the way in which counsellors can become aware of and use their influence base with each client. It is important that you notice and deal appropriately with any signs that your client may benefit more from her direct relationship with you than from goals and techniques.

The developmentally needed relationship, says Clarkson (1990: 153), 'refers to those aspects of relationship which may have been absent or traumatic for the client at particular periods of his or her childhood and which are supplied or repaired by the psychotherapist usually in a contracted form during the psychotherapy'. Although such therapeutic work is often undertaken with more seriously damaged clients over a long time span, it can also become apparent during brief work that clients are deriving benefits from their relationship with you that are of the 'corrective emotional experience' kind. For example, clients who have had particularly poor relationships with their parents may find in you someone who for the first time really takes them seriously, or who shows them ordinary human concern and respect. While the presenting concerns may have been 'focal' (e.g. bulimia) the client may realise during counselling that she is sensing something she has previously missed out on – understanding and concern. Some clients, for example, will ask for hugs, or will want to engage in a certain amount of 'small talk', perhaps because they had very little of these when they were children. Be sensitive to the possibility that such requests sometimes represent new discoveries to some clients; they may never have been able to ask for these things before.

Should aspects of the 'transpersonal relationship' become apparent during counselling, recognise these and respect them. Sometimes you may be aware of an additional, spiritual dimension in your work with some clients. Don't ignore this or consign it to the category of pathology (although some clients, and some counsellors, sometimes try to cover up their personal suffering by involvement in this area of interest). If spirituality becomes an issue, decide together on whether you can profitably work with it within your present, brief contract, and be prepared to renegotiate if necessary. If you have such an interest, for example if you are familiar with analytical psychology, psychosynthesis or other spiritually oriented approaches, you may decide that it is appropriate to work in this area. Or you may decide to refer your client on to practitioners who do work in this way, or to a priest or other suitable helper. Heron (1990) refers to the 'transpersonal process cue' which may alert you to the breakthrough of an 'altered state of consciousness'. (The client may suddenly look very different, sit differently, or use spontaneous new imagery, for example.) Most clients do not seek brief counselling in order to explore such states, but it is possible that some clients, having benefited from a certain amount of groundwork in counselling, will spontaneously enter such states. Be aware then, that the counselling relationship can in some cases engender various needs and experiences which were not 'bargained for' at the outset.

* Summary: Be mindful of how your relationship affects clients. While some may be very goal-directed, others may benefit from the respect and concern you give them. Some clients may experience new states of being following initial counselling. Decide on whether you will work with these, renegotiate your contract, or refer on.

---

64   Explore possible areas of mutual unawareness; refer to supervision

---

You may become conscious during the middle phase not only that your client avoids certain subjects but that you, too, draw away from some subjects. Or you may be vaguely, uneasily half-aware that something is not being addressed. There can be a variety of reasons for such an occurrence. It may be that you have allowed a certain culture of cosiness to develop between you, for example, which is hard to change. Sometimes you may have clients you particularly like, or who remind you of close friends. These occurrences are aspects of countertransference (which can be anything the counsellor feels strongly towards or about the client: see Rowan 1989; Watkins 1989). In such cases you do not always immediately realise that something is amiss. You seem to get on well with the client and the client gets on well with you: both of you are gratified and view this as self-evident progress in counselling.

One way to probe such occurrences is to ask your client directly, 'Do you think there is anything that we haven't discussed and that might be of importance?' If you are aware that the relationship has become cosy, you might try saying, 'We seem to get on very well here, and that may be fine, but *sometimes* it can be a sign of things becoming too easy. Do you have any thoughts on that?' Notice whether, in considering asking such questions, you tend to shy away from them, preferring to leave things as they are. If you do, ask yourself what need you may have to keep things cosy. Have you let the counselling slide into a comforting relationship instead of a working one? And if so, what might you be afraid of if you do confront the client with some difficult issues?

If you have been tape-recording sessions, then you can listen to your tapes with such questions in mind. Better still, you can play them to your supervisor and ask for feedback on the tone of your interventions. Are there signs that you are backing away from challenging the client and making life (in counselling) easy for yourself and your client? It is easier for you to ask yourself this question if you are at least dimly aware of something of the kind seeping into your counselling. However, this phenomenon can be made all the harder to detect if you are unconsciously presenting your work with certain clients as non-problematic. Trainee counsellors often say in supervision, for example, 'Oh, I haven't got much to say this week; there are no problems with my client.' Or you may not present a certain client for supervision. This selectivity may well be unconscious, but it is sometimes an indicator of a degree of unawareness. For this reason (among others) Windy often asks trainees to bring all their tapes to supervision for him to make a 'lucky dip'. A willingness to expose any and all of your work is a good way to avoid this kind of problem from taking root. Even without using such tactics, your supervisor is there as another set of eyes and ears and can offer fresh perspectives on work which you are missing.

* Summary: Look out for any signs of overly comfortable or cosy relationships with any of your clients. Watch for any reluctance on your part to be challenging. Monitor all your work for such instances and take all cases to supervision.

---

65   Be alert to your client's dependency on counselling and on you as a counsellor; help clients to orientate themselves towards personal confidence and autonomous growth

---

Although you will have discussed with your client the nature of brief counselling, and you may have already discussed termination, she may nevertheless show signs of clinging to the counselling relationship or to you. There is a difference between a certain level of intimacy and liking, and a more dysfunctional level of dependence. We also recognise that some clients need to learn to become intimate and not to remain aloof from their counsellor or terminate too prematurely. But here we are focusing on the kind of client who you will recognise as wanting to make counselling and the counsellor the centre of her world.

Sometimes this is a sign that there is little between-session work going on. If your client turns up for sessions saying, 'I've been thinking about this problem and wondering what you'll think about it', this can be an indication that you are becoming her guru, or a substitute for her making her own efforts to change. In such a case, try responding, 'What do you think I would've said if I'd been there?' Encourage the client to own the learning she has acquired and to practise it in her everyday life. Do not be drawn again and again into the role of the wise consultant. As Sheldon Kopp (1974) advised clients, 'If you meet the Buddha on the road, kill him'. By this he meant that it is dangerous to invest too much faith in apparently omniscient others, since it erodes your own personal learning. You don't have to respond to such questions with a wooden, 'You'd like me to tell you what to do'. Remind the client of the work you have done together, and the themes you have been working on; encourage her to do her own work. Ask the client 'What would I have said or done in that situation?' But then ask the client to consult her own 'inner counsellor' (by which we mean her own decision-making processes). Encourage her to re-create a scene in which a problem presented itself, and in which she relied on some idea of what you or other 'wise' people in her life would have done or said, and ask her to create a different solution of her own.

Reinforce the agreement that counselling is to be brief. Let your client know that she is capable. When your client conveys the idea that she is too weak to cope on her own, or hasn't yet learned sufficient skills to entertain the idea of ending counselling, consider changing the pattern of sessions. 'Well, let's see if that's true. Shall we test it out? I suggest we might schedule a break of two weeks, say, and see how you get on.' In this way, clients can empirically test the idea that they cannot cope without you or counselling. (We are assuming here that there is no genuine crisis involved.) It may even come to the point, towards termination, that your client claims not to be able to continue without you, or insists that she have more sessions. Simon Budman demonstrates (in Budman and Gurman 1988: 362) that it is sometimes necessary to argue your case with some degree of force for not offering further sessions. Should you encounter such resistance, it is useful to be able to state clearly why you consider time-limited counselling to be appropriate. Part of your statement should reinforce the client's coping abilities and the idea that gains in counselling continue to operate afterwards. Remind the client that counselling is a tool to help with better living. In doing this, it is necessary that you believe what you are saying! It may be that in some cases you will decide to refer the client on for long-term therapy.

* **Summary: Look for signs that clients are becoming overly dependent on the counselling process or on you as a counsellor. Check that they are putting what they learn into everyday practice. Suggest breaks in schedule to allow the client to test out whether or not they use what they have learned from counselling in their lives.**

---

66   Be alert to any deterioration in your client's condition and respond appropriately

---

A small percentage of clients may, as counselling progresses into the middle phase, show signs of worsening. There can be a temptation, for example, when a previously tense and expressionless client starts to break down and cry, to regard some forms of distress as indications of therapeutic progress; sometimes that is the case. But there is also a danger that some people get into a pattern of regression, crying, writhing, 'somatising' (e.g. getting many headaches) etc. that should not be regarded as routine signs of 'getting in touch with feelings'.

Mays and Franks's (1985) study of 'negative outcomes' in therapy listed many signs of deterioration as a result of therapist errors. These signs included depressive breakdown; destructive acting out; increased anxiety; exaggeration of somatic difficulties; increased guilt or confusion; lower self-esteem. Colson et al. (1985: 72) suggested that 'therapists or analysts were often slow to recognise the negative-outcome patients' actual personal and treatment needs and to shift treatment approach accordingly, from tactics suitable for an expressive psychotherapy to a more highly structured and supportive approach'. If your way of working particularly utilises challenging and uncovering interventions, you need to take extra care at the assessment stage, to monitor the reactions of all clients, and to be well supervised. Look out for any tendency you may have to want to push clients overly hard. Don't let the excitement of eliciting dramatic abreactions, for example, blind you to the possibility that your client (and you) may be getting too deeply, too early, into chaotic and painful material. If this happens inadvertently, respond by offering more structure (more talking-through of problems and feelings, more specific monitoring of daily moods, etc.).

While some clients fail to make due progress because their counsellors are not skilful or potent enough, others deteriorate because their counsellors are too therapeutically ambitious. Know your own limitations and those of your clients. When clients become rapidly distressed, or frequently distressed, or often confused, take this to supervision, but also consider making use of other resources. In the case of severely depressed clients, for example, it may not be enough to ask them to 'close the escape hatches' (Stewart 1989). Consider getting psychiatric advice; advise the client to consult a GP; consider making a referral to another counsellor or therapist. Although some counsellors have an anti-medication stance, some clients are helped by anti-depressants, for example, and such medication can often be used in conjunction with counselling. Familiarise yourself with local and specialist resources. Learn to identify which clients show signs of deterioration under which conditions. Overcome any anxieties you may have regarding your own professional status: if you have doubts about your ability to deal with particular clients, discuss these with your supervisor and do not hesitate to make a referral.

* **Summary: Heed any signs from clients that they are getting worse in counselling. Do not confound exhibitions of deep feelings with obvious progress. Monitor such cases carefully, taking them to supervision and if necessary referring them on.**

67 Deal with any crises that may arise

If you are counselling someone over a period of months, it may well be that life events will arise which distress or preoccupy your client. They may very well cut across the work you are doing. Suppose that you are working with a client on an eating disorder, and a friend of hers is suddenly involved in a fatal accident. Your client will probably want to spend time grieving, and integrating the impact of this event into her life. It is quite likely that such an event will temporarily become more important to your client than her previous concerns. (This is assuming that your client is not in such a critical state herself that her own welfare should take precedence over an accidental event concerning someone else.)

Significant life events during the course of counselling can dramatically alter its outcome (for better or for worse). Respond sensitively and appropriately to such events. You may need to check with your client that she wishes to alter the contract at such a time. 'It seems that you need time to talk about this. Shall we put aside what we had planned, and return to it when you feel the time is right?' Do not make assumptions about how upset or not the client will be, but watch for non-verbal signals of denied grief or other reactions.

Some fortuitous events may represent crises for counselling but not, apparently, for the client. Suppose that your client suddenly wins quite a lot of money, is elated, and feels that her problems have evaporated – what will you do? It may well be appropriate to agree with the client that she seems relieved, happily preoccupied and not in need of any further counselling at present. But you would be wise to suggest that the present elation may not last and that you will be available should she wish to return at a later time.

Another category of crisis is sometimes seen in clients who are accident-prone or histrionic. In such cases the crisis may not be 'real', or it may be unconsciously 'created' by the client. You may not meet such clients very often, but some, who have what has come to be known as a 'personality disorder', for example, will create crises in order to get attention. Or some clients may 'hit bottom' during counselling and inflict harm on themselves. At times like these you will need to consider seriously whether you can continue with your contract, or if there is a need for referral. But what you cannot do is ignore such events. In the case of clients who regularly present with 'crises', you need to feed this back to them and to consider if brief counselling can proceed if clients have little or no insight into their behaviour.

* Summary: Pay attention to genuine crises and check that your clients receive from you, or get elsewhere, the support they need to deal with them. Be aware of the varieties of crisis that can occur and of how they may require quite different handling.

---

68   Evaluate progress and deal with any disappointment that the client has regarding the rate of progress

You may become conscious of the client's (or your own) enthusiasm flagging during the middle phase. It may feel as if counselling sessions are becoming something of a ritual. Take such signs seriously and instigate a review of progress. Some counsellors suggest formal review sessions as a matter of course, and this is a practice to be commended, provided that it is not allowed to become an empty ritual of mutual congratulation. But what do you look for in either formal or informal evaluation discussions?

Check on actual progress regarding agreed goals. Have they been reached partially or fully? What obstacles remain to achieving them? Beyond individual goals, to what extent has progress been made with the client's underlying constructs? For example, if the client's goals related to becoming less anxious, how has she achieved this? Has she learned to identify, say, her irrational beliefs and how to challenge them? Where has she come to at this stage in counselling and what remains for her to achieve? In what ways does she find you helpful and unhelpful? How can you offer more appropriate help?

Evaluation is both quantitative and qualitative. It may be on-going, if you have developed the habit of constantly referring to the reflection process, or it may be scheduled in as a formal pro-cedure. Sutton (1989) is a proponent of precise client measure-ments of change in counselling. Such measurements cannot be taken unless you and your client agreed clear and unmistak-able goals at the outset, which include what she wished to achieve and how she would know when she had achieved it. Simple graphs can be used for this purpose (see Appendix 6). Ryle (1990) has built into his model a variety of evaluation procedures for both client and counsellor.

We are aware that many counsellors dislike the notion of evaluation, or at least of formal evaluation of progress. In the humanistic 'camp', Rowan (1989: 171) gives a 'list of criteria for doing good therapy' which some counsellors may find compat-ible with their approach and useful as a means of evaluating their work. Person-centred counsellors are unlikely to engage in formal evaluation unless the client requests it, yet may be very aware of the progress their clients have made (or not made) ac-cording to Rogers's (1990) 'seven stages of process'. Rogers's process continuum begins with clients perceiving themselves and events in fixed terms and ends with clients appreciating the nuances of their own feelings and the choices before them. Rogers's view was that these stages could be evidenced in time-limited therapy (he cites Lewis et al. 1959) and it seems, therefore, that even person-centred evaluation of counselling progress is quite practical. To some extent, how you structure evaluation of client progress is a matter of taste. You might also measure results against Prochaska and DiClemente's (1984) stages of change. If your client has moved from contemplation to action or main-tenance on certain target concerns, then progress is clear. When evaluating, be sure to involve your client as fully as possible and to clarify which points you agree and do not agree on.

At this stage you may learn that your client is disappointed with the rate of progress. This can either signify that change has indeed been slow and very modest (and that it relates to client motivation or counsellor interventions) or that the client has harboured unrealistic fantasies of change. You need to check these possibilities carefully. Garfield (1989) advocates explicit discus-sion of such disappointment. It is often the case, he argues, that the way in which clients deal with (or even set up) disappoint-ments, reflects other similar phenomena in their lives. This is not a licence to dismiss valid criticisms of your counselling, however: do heed what clients tell you about your counselling style. Garfield (1989: 100) also suggests that 'if the therapist is seeing a client who meets the general criteria of being a suitable candidate for brief psychotherapy and there is no discernible progress after five or six interviews, the therapist should attempt some evaluation of the case'. Caution needs to be taken that you neither try to hurry inappropriately in such cases, nor overlook possible causes of non-improvement.

* Summary: Either look for signs that an evaluation of counselling progress is called for, or initiate a formal review session. Consider ways in which you and the client can evaluate progress, including ongoing reflection and formal written assessments. Use baseline measurements that suit your approach and your client's needs. Deal with client disappointment.

---

69 Be prepared to renegotiate goals where it becomes apparent that presenting concerns concealed other problems

---

In counselling and psychotherapy the client's material can often, of course, be other than what it seems. We do not think that brief counsellors are, or should be, any less aware of this than long-term practitioners. However, in working focally there is a concentration on certain material and a risk, therefore, of over-looking other concerns. Both consciously and unconsciously, clients sometimes conceal or de-emphasise certain matters, which may surface later in the counselling process.

At a conscious level clients may occasionally decide 'not to bother you' with certain matters; they may be aware of something painful that they cannot bring themselves to discuss immediately; or they may lie to you. In cases where clients disclose to you that there is something on their mind which they have not discussed before, listen carefully to this new material and help the client to decide what priority to give it in counselling. In cases where clients tell you that they have concealed something, show your interest and concern non-judgmentally. Ask whether there is anything in your manner which has made it difficult for them to tell you before. Be ready to set new goals with the client if the

new material is critical, and discuss whether it fits in with the
approach you have been using.

An example of a fortuitous discovery of concealed problems is
given by John Marzillier (in Dryden 1992). Marzillier was using
behavioural methods with a client whose problem was a difficulty in urinating in public conveniences. In order to help the
client, Marzillier accompanied him to a pub where the client had
to drink enough to be able to urinate in the public toilet. While
he and Marzillier were drinking and waiting for the drink to pass
through the client's system, they talked informally (and without
design) about the client's life, his family difficulties and career
dilemma. Marzillier reports that progress with the urination
problem was slow and the client left treatment to travel abroad.
By chance they met two years later, and Marzillier was surprised
to discover that the client first failed to remember the (urination)
problem, and then admitted that it was still in evidence, but of
no great consequence. The lessons of this reflection are that our
intentions and methods are not always appropriate and that
clients sometimes have more important underlying problems or
preoccupations. Some psychodynamic practitioners insist that
problems invariably have deeper, underlying dynamics which
must be addressed. While this is obviously not our position in
this book, we suggest that you remain aware of unexpressed under-
currents in your client's material.

What may happen when previously undisclosed matters are
brought out at this stage is that the client will ask for more time.
What was apparently a straightforward fear of going on under-
ground trains, for example, turns out to relate to sexual abuse in
childhood. In such an instance, what will you do? Unless there is
a very good reason, don't change your original brief contract into
a completely open-ended arrangement. If appropriate, agree to
lengthen the work with your client, but first discuss this issue in
supervision. Sometimes there is a compelling case for such ex-
tended work, as in this example. But sometimes clients will resist
the termination of counselling and create dependency by producing
urgent new reasons for being given more time. Discuss all such
cases in supervision to ensure that you are not being drawn into
a collusive relationship with your client. To take the same case
of sexual abuse, your decision to continue to work with this client
may include questioning your knowledge and ability in working
in this area. It may be appropriate to refer the client on. In various examples of clients discovering hidden material and getting
into deeper areas of intrapsychic distress than they and you had

anticipated, consider the appropriateness of referring on to counsellors or psychotherapists who work more at this level.

* Summary: Be aware of new material surfacing in counselling and of any necessity to negotiate new goals accordingly. Question whether you can offer what your client needs, whether you can change your approach, or if there is a need to refer on. Do not automatically slip into open-ended work.

---

70 Help the client to understand the non-linear nature of change

---

Change in counselling is rarely, if ever, smooth and uni-directional. It can commonly include elements of hesitancy, enthusiasm, sustained commitment, 'conversion', stuckness, 'peak experiences', disappointments, incidental learning, crises, relapses and stable maintenance. Yet clients quite often hope for or expect dramatic, rapid and irreversible changes. The degree of fantasy involved may be directly related to the amount of suffering in the client's past. The reality is that counselling can be a rough ride, with ups, downs, and times of backsliding. Explain this to your client at an appropriate time, and explain that this is a universal experience rather than only true of them.

A model of non-linear change that may be useful to consider is that given by Windy (Dryden 1990). This includes the three dimensions of frequency, duration and intensity. Ask your client if he experiences his distress or difficulty more or less often than previously (frequency). Likewise, when the distress occurs, does it last as long as it used to do or a shorter time (duration)? When it occurs, is the distress as intense as before, less so or more so (intensity)? Help the client to be specific in identifying these factors. Often it is useful to have her record these items on paper, especially if she is anxious about progress. Such recording is a systematic feature in cognitive-analytic therapy, where clients are encouraged to rate their progress on target problems on a weekly or similarly regular basis.

Prochaska and DiClemente (1984) view the change process as circular rather than linear. Particularly in relation to clients with addictive problems, but also in relation to clients broadly, they speak of a 'revolving door' model of change. Depending on the stage of change at which they enter counselling and at which they terminate or drop-out, clients will often proceed in circles of change, re-entering the sequence of contemplation, action and maintenance, for example, until stability is progressively achieved. Even without dropping out of counselling, clients may 'go in circles' of contemplation and action from session to session.

* **Summary: Explain to your clients that progress is rarely the smooth affair that they would wish it to be. Encourage them to monitor their own progress on each target concern. Get across the message that non-linear change is the norm.**

---

71   Recognise and deal with any impasses

Impasses (stubborn obstacles) can occur at any stage of counselling but often occur most frequently in the middle stage. It has been noted of organisations as well as individuals that there is an in-built conservatism. People wish to change but simultaneously experience a wish to remain the same; what is familiar is reassuring and what is unknown often evokes fear or wariness. When your clients reach a certain stage in their counselling, the easier goals may have been reached and more challenging goals may present themselves and invoke anxiety or resistance. Such impasses as may result from this resistance can relate to the client–counsellor relationship or to clients' relationship with their tasks and everyday life. Impasses can also come from, or be exacerbated by, your countertransference (the attitudes you have towards your clients, of which you may not be fully aware). Some counsellors believe in staying with impasses, and in using the core conditions of counselling gradually to erode them; others find it more helpful to employ deliberate strategies. Consider various examples of impasses.

The client will not work actively
or confront feared obstacles

Ask the client if he understands the tasks required of him in counselling. Does he think he can perform them and that they will be effective in achieving his aims? He may have appeared to understand and agree with you but is not really convinced, and hence seems stubborn. Does he, perhaps, believe that progress should come easily, that counselling is a passive and receptive exercise? Confronted with a need to make effort and experience some discomfort, does he have an attitude of low frustration tolerance (meaning that he believes that he cannot tolerate the discomfort)? Are you pushing him too quickly or too soon? Look at the possibilities of obstacles on both your side and his. Consider, too, using an 'advantages and disadvantages of maintaining/ changing the present behaviour' inventory (Appendix 5). This kind of exercise can help to demonstrate to the client his perceptions and beliefs regarding the good aspects of not changing and the bad aspects of changing, in both the short and longer term.

The client is overly concerned about his relationship with you

Sometimes clients will draw you into social conversation, wanting to know all about your week, your thoughts, your own experiences, and so on. Many clients experience their counsellors as 'the only person who ever really listened to me' or 'the only person who really knows me'. This can lead to a mistaken focus on the counsellor. Skilful psychodynamic counsellors will interpret such instances of transference. But there is often the possibility that clients secretly regard you as their salvation, and consequently do not stretch themselves in their everyday life. Remind clients that the purpose of counselling is personal change, which involves dealing with their own concerns inside and outside the counselling-room. Find your own way of keeping your client focused on his tasks. This can conclude work with the transference. It can also entail a practice of discouraging social niceties. Mahrer (1989), for example, discourages what he sees as the dysfunctional 'role relationship' of counsellor and client by getting straight into the work; by sitting parallel with the client, with closed eyes; and by focusing entirely on the client's inner experiencing.

The client focuses on others and on circumstances

Some clients talk a lot about their partners, their jobs, the weather, their holidays, and so on; some clients tell you how awful their partners or bosses are; or how terrible their childhood was. There is often a lot of truth in these accounts, but not necessarily truth that can be useful. The clients are in counselling to effect changes for themselves. Remind them of that. The people in their life cannot be changed. Sometimes clients blame circumstances rather than accept personal responsibility, because then they might believe that they have to blame themselves. In some cases you have clients who experience great difficulty in not talking incessantly about other people and circumstances: it is probably their habitual style of talking, or it may reflect anxiety about change. As we have mentioned earlier, you may need to interrupt conversation of this kind and to educate such clients into the appropriate role of a client in counselling.

You and the client get into a transference–countertransference entanglement

There may be occasions in every counselling relationship where some transference and/or countertransference is operating. Where it is obviously one-way it can be dealt with either by the counsellor's vigilance and interpretation, or by resort to supervision. But when there is simultaneously strong transference and countertransference, you may experience difficulties. Suppose that you and your client begin to get angry or irritable with each other, in the sense of 'getting on the wrong side of each other'; perhaps it becomes hard to maintain very much adult-to-adult communication; or perhaps there are simply times when the relationship becomes clearly difficult. In such cases, definitely take this to supervision. But also deal with it by referring to the reflection process. Discover if there is anything you have done which has offended your client or triggered off strong feelings in the client. Remember that it is more your responsibility than the client's to maintain a mature adult perspective. If you notice that you become defensive, watch this and step outside it. It is quite appropriate to apologise to clients if you have made an error, for example. Encourage clients to move into their 'observing ego' at these times, by showing empathy.

You experience overpowering (e.g. erotic) countertransference

Countertransference takes many forms and in its most unhelpful form needs to be dealt with by the counsellor's own therapy and supervision. But it also provides useful information about the client. In the case of an erotic countertransference (which is, we believe, far more common than people realise) you need to learn to distinguish between what comes from you, what comes from the client, and what is mutual. If you are distracted by such feelings towards your client, there is a problem. If, after discussing this in supervision, you cannot make progress with it, you may have to consider referring your client elsewhere. But first, consider whether there is any way in which your client elicits these feelings, and where you think this may be the case, share this sensitively with the client. Don't 'blame' the client for it, but ask whether he or she is aware of strong feelings between you. Some counsellors, particularly those who can confidently be themselves in the counselling process, may bring these feelings into the open and make good therapeutic use of them. If you are in doubt about your ability to do this, put it aside until you have discussed it in supervision. Feelings of this kind are understandable; where they become intrusive or overpowering, you need to think hard. Don't berate yourself for having them, but don't keep them to yourself either.

You and the client get into a collusively superficial relationship

You may sometimes be tempted to take it easy with a particular client. Perhaps you feel that someone is too fragile to push in the beginning, so you hold off, and the holding off becomes a pattern that is hard to break. Perhaps you like the client and have a similar background; and therefore you value their company. Or, as a beginning counsellor, you may experience an anxiety to keep the client. It can be a natural temptation, after losing one client because you were 'too hard', to react by being very soft and unchallenging. In all such instances, remind yourself that this is not, after all, a social relationship and that non-possessive warmth does not mean 'being nice' to clients. You and they are meeting together to effect concrete changes in clients' attitudes and lives.

* Summary: Impasses can manifest in various ways. Look for signs that your client is more focused on you, others or circumstances, than on personal change. In cases where you and your client arouse strong feelings in each other, be sure to discuss this in supervision and if necessary to consider referral elsewhere if these feelings cannot be contained or used therapeutically.

PART VI
Ending counselling

72 Initiate preparation for termination

In the introduction to his book, Flegenheimer (1982) quotes from Malan (who is echoing Samuel Johnson): 'Being under sentence of termination doth most marvelously concentrate the material'. In other words, in brief therapy many practitioners capitalise on the fact that clients know that they do not have all the time in the world. They are aware from the very beginning that they had better focus on their concerns and maintain their motivation. Some counsellors will emphasise this 'sentence of termination' at the contracting stage in order to ensure that there is no misunderstanding. Indeed, some practitioners use a 'countdown' system of reminding clients at each session of how many sessions have gone by and how many remain. We are aware that such a practice is disliked by many counsellors, but it is practised successfully by many counsellors working from psychodynamic, behavioural and other perspectives.

Budman and Gurman (1988) make a point of reminding clients that counselling is not the centre of their lives and that learning goes on apart from counselling and after it. Termination is thus close to the surface throughout the counselling process. We noted, earlier, differences between time-limited, brief and open-ended counselling. However, if you are working within a brief counselling contract, there will often be no countdown and therefore no explicit awareness of termination to come. There is sometimes a temptation to let the subject of termination slide. We suggest that you raise the subject and keep it appropriately alive. One direct way of challenging clients' objections that they cannot possibly think about termination, is to raise the reality issue that counsellors sometimes move jobs: what would your client do if you moved to another part of the country?

When is the best time to raise this subject? Obviously timing will depend on individual circumstances. In general (in non-time-limited counselling) you would do well to be sensitive to signs that the counselling process has firmly gotten underway before talking much about termination. Perhaps after your client has achieved significant progress with two or three goals, you might allude to increased hope for a better future. Don't get into a clumsy attempt to persuade your clients that they are ready to consider termination when they are clearly distressed or averse to discussing ending. But, equally, don't put the subject off indefinitely. Some clients, particularly those who are highly motivated or whose problems are well-defined, may positively invite discussion of termination. They may see it as encouraging, as confirming the manageability of their problems and as showing them 'the light at the end of the tunnel'. If your clients are at the action or maintenance stages we have discussed earlier, they may welcome discussion of termination because they may well want to make and consolidate progress fairly quickly.

Kupers (1988) has looked closely at the subject of termination in both short- and long-term therapies. He concludes that termination is a complex issue and that in practical terms clients often move from one therapy experience to another anyway, thus making strict definitions of termination difficult. Amada (1983) suggests that many brief therapies, beginning with an apparently well-defined problem focus, actually become long-term when it is evident that clients are seeking deeper and more open-ended therapeutic exploration. Our view is that this apparent openness to clients' needs, this flexibility between brief and long-term approaches, had better be scrutinised very carefully. When you initiate discussion of termination with clients, listen to how you present it. Are you convinced that an end is in sight? Do you think that (relatively) brief work with this client is truly appropriate? Are you beginning to like this client, and to be fascinated by her intricate psychological world? Is your client subtly signalling to you that her distress is deeper than you had thought? Is she forming an attachment to you and, if so, is that attachment a necessary and valuable part of a therapeutic process? Or is it a dependency on you and a partial avoidance of the hard work of personal change?

Colin saw a client in a community counselling setting which attempts to limit the number of sessions, for practical reasons. The client first applied for counselling when in crisis. By the time she could be seen the crisis had passed, but there was still some useful work to be done which related, broadly, to assertiveness. She made very good progress, working actively between sessions to put what she learned in counselling into practice. I initiated discussion of termination by telling her, 'I think you've moved a lot from your original position. Each time we meet you've gained more ground for yourself, and the future looks very promising. What do you think you can get from further counselling that you can't do for yourself?' She replied that coming to counselling felt supportive and helped her to concentrate on her goals. I accepted this response and agreed that we would continue to meet for a few more weeks. But I also had a sense that I had become a social focus for her. Many clients find in their counsellors 'the only person I can really talk to'. This is not, in the short term, a bad thing, perhaps, but it can too easily come to complicate the end of counselling. This particular client would probably have continued counselling indefinitely, for very mixed motives, had I not persistently reminded her of a need to terminate (for example, by reminding her of why she first came, of how much she had achieved, and by affirming a belief in the time-limited nature of the counselling on offer in that particular setting). She finally agreed to a tapering-off method of coming to an end.

* **Summary: With appropriate timing, introduce the subject of the inevitability and desirability of counselling coming to an end. Explain the advantages of concentrated work, and in doing so examine your own attitudes to termination issues.**

---

73   Promote self-change

We have advocated an approach to counselling that is active for both client and counsellor, yet in the beginning stages you will have provided a lot of the input yourself. Guard against letting this activity take over. Once you feel confident that your clients have substantially grasped and internalised new ways of looking at and dealing with their problems, prepare to hand over the reins of counselling and of change to them.

When the time has come for this switch from counsellor to client 'leadership', the client is probably at the stage of maintenance (Prochaska and DiClemente 1984). She needs to secure her gains, experiment with them, apply them to different situations and to make the learning resources for progress her own. Egan (1990) suggests that clients at this stage need 'social support and challenge'. In other words, in order to maintain their progress, they will be helped by reinforcement of their goals from friends, as well as necessary challenge and stimulation. People who have gone through treatment programmes for alcoholism, for example, are often actively encouraged to attend regular meetings of Alcoholics Anonymous. Maintenance implies a careful watch over progress made so far. When we speak of promoting self-change we are not referring to a naive endorsement of positive thinking (e.g. 'You don't need this counselling. All you need to do is go out there and get on with life. You can do it if you really want to.'). Don't send your clients on a 'flight into health' but encourage them gradually to continue their journey independently.

There are various means of offering such encouragement. One is the in-session exercise of 'rational role reversal' (Dryden 1982). In this exercise you ask your client to take the role of the counsellor, while you take up the role of the client. Your client challenges 'your' cognitive errors and assists you in finding better perspectives on her problems. In taking such a lead, she experiences the more rational and coping part of herself, and actively confronts her own doubts. Another way of preparing for self-change is to ask your client to visualise you, her counsellor, sitting on her shoulder, talking to her, whenever she encounters difficulties in everyday life. This is, in effect, offering a 'transitional object' to the client. At those times when she is unsure of her new-found abilities, she may be comforted and helped by the image and memory of you and of the kind of approach you have used together. You can elaborate on this exercise by using the image of a magic lamp that the client rubs in times of difficulty: her counsellor issues from the lamp and she is able to engage in an imaginal consultation. We do stress that such exercises will help some clients better than others, and that they are only interim measures – they are not the ultimate aim of counselling!

Let's look at how you might help clients take on the idea of self-change:

You: OK, now we've been talking about how you felt at the bus-stop and at your evening class. What do you think is the common link here?

Client: Well, in both cases I suppose I was embarrassed. I felt as if I'd made a fool of myself.

You: From what we've discussed together, what can you identify in this connection that you might work on?

Client: I was embarrassed. The embarrassment was a feeling of . . . I was thinking 'they're looking at me, expecting me to say something friendly, and I can't; they must think I'm stupid'. Something like that.

You: Take that further.

Client: They may not have thought anything of the kind. There wasn't any evidence of that, no. I automatically expected them to think that when I fumbled for words . . . and I suppose I set myself up for feeling bad.

You: And even if they had thought that . . .?

Client: I wouldn't *have* to feel embarrassed. I could think 'I wonder what they're thinking', or I could ask them, or even if I got embarrassed, that's uncomfortable but not intolerable.

In this dialogue, the counsellor is prompting the client to remember previous work together. Instead of doing the interim steps for her, he provides cues and leaves her to work out the process herself. She may not do it as he would do it, but in this instance he wants her to see that she can do it to some extent. She arrives at an array of options. Feeling acutely embarrassed is not inevitable for her. This process could have gone on, perhaps, to look at how she might dispute with herself when another problematic situation arises. But this is a first step.

How do you promote self-change when you are using other models? Ryle's (1990) cognitive-analytic therapy has built-in self-change assignments (questionnaires, written and other tasks) and is strictly time-limited. We have already looked closely at the whole subject of homework in Part IV (Sections 41–60), but here it is worth noting that Macaskill (1985: 140) argues 'that homework assignments are conceptually and technically consistent with current models of brief dynamic psychotherapy and, furthermore, that setting homework assignments offers substantial therapeutic benefits in terms of maintaining a focus, evolving a sound therapeutic alliance, enhancing motivation and reducing termination difficulties'. Analytically oriented counsellors may have a particular interest in the ways in which some clients resist the notion of self-change. There is a difference between understanding such resistance, of course, and helping the client to overcome it. In the context of brief counselling you cannot afford to let your client slowly work through such resistance. Ryle's model (in common with other brief psychodynamic models) discourages the forming of fantasies of eternal dependence on the counsellor.

* Summary: Progressively encourage clients to take over the process of change. Show them how to internalise what they have learned already. Use various exercises if they are helpful to your clients. Demonstrate how the approach you have used together can be used *in situ*. Reflect on your own orientation and the weight you place on clients' independence.

74   Address the subject of relapse prevention

While the engendering of hope is an important part of counselling, addressing the likelihood of relapse is perhaps just as
important. Relapse is the full or partial return to a previous,
undesired level of functioning. As we have already noted, change
is rarely, if ever, linear. It is much more often a matter of a
great many advances and a great many (minor or major) relapses.
By now you may well have introduced the subject to your
client.

Since you are concerned that clients will maintain their gains
after counselling, you need to address possible future pitfalls
now, while there is still time and commitment from the client.
Bring this subject up with an awareness of the client's stage
of change. If the client is at the contemplative stage, it is inappropriate, of course. But when the client has made changes and
perhaps consolidated some of them, it may be time to introduce
the subject. 'What can you foresee that might stop you from
maintaining these gains?' you might ask. 'I'm really keen to see
you develop your gains even further and I'm wondering what
possible obstacles might lie in your path in the future' is another
way to put it. Discussion of relapse and its prevention is not a
matter of painting a gloomy scenario but of being realistic and
prepared.

Having established with your client that relapse is a common
experience for most people in counselling, explain the significance of anticipating its occurrence. Ask the client to imagine
and identify what obstacles in himself, in others and in his
circumstances might contribute towards relapse. Help him to
visualise the kinds of setting in which he might be tempted to
succumb to his former habit, or to abandon his new set of beliefs.
Who might assist him in his future downfall? What little signs
might there be that relapse is imminent? Actively encourage him
to use imagery to foresee relapse situations. Introduce the idea of
rehearsal for possible relapse and its management. Suggest to the
client that relapse is not awful and in fact is an opportunity to
test the reality of his gains in counselling. If appropriate, actively
encourage the client to seek out situations in which he will be
tested. Show him how to use such situations as cues for problem-
solving.

There are objections to a relapse prevention intervention. Some people claim that it dampens hope. Indeed, there are conditions that are so stubborn (particularly addictions) that counsellors working in those fields may rely on a vision of complete abstinence, emphasising a 'one day at a time' approach. This vision seems to stem from the idea that even to contemplate the possibility of relapse is almost to invite it. We agree that addictions like alcoholism and drug abuse are serious and stubborn problems. However, Marlatt and Gordon (1985) have to some extent countered this argument with their concept of the 'abstinence violation effect' (AVE). When someone has remained abstinent from alcohol for a long time, and then one day drinks a glass of wine, they may tell themselves that they've completely messed up all the progress they made; they berate themselves, feel terrible and drink all the more in order to overcome the resulting bad feelings. They may also rationalise, using the 'I may as well be hung for a sheep as for a lamb' argument. Marlatt and Gordon teach that such 'slips' are small, understandable and forgivable instances of human error. They are not reasons for 'awfulising', to use a concept from rational-emotive therapy. Note that we are not saying that it is fine to be blasé about clients reverting to their undesirable behaviour. We simply advocate that it be kept in proportion and not be used to make matters even worse.

Using the above example, you might run through this eventuality with a client, having him imagine that drink. Do so as if it were happening in the present to make the experience come alive. What are the circumstances leading up to it? What thoughts run through his mind at the time? What does he tell himself as he does it? How does the problem escalate? What might he do or think differently that would lead to a different outcome? Don't convey the idea that relapse is acceptable, but that instances of it (behaviourally or in experiences of temptation) are likely to occur. Be sensitive to the individual client, his level of understanding and 'ego strength'. Gauge the time and the means for addressing the subject of relapse. Explain to clients that there is often a movement to greater control and better coping skills over time (Prochaska and DiClemente 1984).

* Summary: Appropriately and sensitively introduce clients to the subject of relapse and to the likelihood of its occurring. Demonstrate the importance of anticipation and rehearsal. Use imagery and cognitive restructuring to prepare for relapse. Convey the idea that relapse is not the end of the world, but a chance to test problem-solving skills.

---

75   Respect the right of a client who wishes to terminate abruptly to do so

---

Some counsellors believe that there is an ideal way for clients to
end their counselling. We do not. We look at different kinds of
endings later, but here we want to convey one of the realities of
counselling, which is that some clients do terminate 'prematurely'. Another way of saying this is that some clients terminate
before their counsellors think they should. Now, if you have
picked up cues earlier in the counselling process that your client
is doubtful about what progress she is making, or dissatisfied in
some other way, you may have had the chance to deal with such
issues. But sometimes there are few cues and you do find that
your client suddenly announces that this is the last session, or
she simply doesn't turn up.

If your client does bring up the subject of ending before you
think it is appropriate, by all means explore her reasons for
wanting to do so. However, do understand the difference between
exploring and coercing. Don't subtly persuade her that she really
does need further counselling when she obviously doesn't want
it. Avoid in any way putting her down or causing bad feelings
when it is clear that she has decided to end. Don't be tempted
to interpret this as a 'flight into health'. What you may do is
convey your understanding, and your willingness to welcome her
back later should she wish to return. Some counsellors make a
point of telling clients well in advance that there may come a
time in counselling when they (the clients) will feel like quitting
because of difficulties they may experience in the counselling
process.

We have both had personal experiences as clients of counsellors and therapists trying to persuade us that our decision to
leave therapy was a misguided and defensive one. Such experiences
can be very upsetting for clients, and particularly so for less
assertive or less informed clients, who may find it difficult to
argue with the counsellor. Counsellors do on occasion have very
strong beliefs about their clients' stage of change in counselling,
and their depth of pathology, that is at odds with their clients'
perceptions. If you find yourself wanting to dissuade your client
of her resolve to terminate, ask yourself to what extent you are
within her, or your own, frame of reference, and whether you are

deriving some special satisfaction from this client. Remind your-self that you have contracted to work collaboratively towards the client's goals, and if you are reasonably sure that your client has achieved her goals or is within sight of them, then you can prepare to end gracefully. If you are not confident that this is the case, use the reflection process to solicit the client's view; if she confirms that she has not, after all, substantially achieved her goals, review your work together, take it to supervision, and consider extending the time you have together or a referral if appropriate. We believe that it is not ethical or appropriate to attempt to keep your client in counselling beyond her wishes. (The only real exception to this would be temporarily holding on to a client who is endangering herself or others.)

When a client terminates abruptly, letting you know either directly or indirectly that she is unhappy with your counselling, don't take it personally. Accept that you may have made a mistake (particularly if you are a beginner) and learn from the experience. Remember that even experienced counsellors have clients who terminate 'prematurely' because the clients do not get on with them. You may, however, need to attend to certain practicalities after termination. If you are unsure whether your client will be returning, we suggest that you write (rather than telephone) in a welcoming manner, letting her know that she can feel free to get in touch. If clients have left owing you money, you will need to send an invoice; in this case, you might say simply that you welcome their contacting you, but in the mean time, here is your invoice. There is no call for any persecutory behaviour! We also suggest that when a client in brief counselling fails to turn up for an appointment, you do not adopt the analytic habit of keeping the space open for the following week: it is unlikely that they will turn up if they have not been in touch. We suggest that you do not make phone calls because these can be intrusive and do not allow the client time to reflect. You may well persuade a client to return, but you will also, perhaps, be undermining their autonomy. If the case ever arises that you need to cancel a ses-sion, you should consider this in advance and seek the client's permission to phone or make alternative arrangements.

* Summary: Deal sensitively with clients who terminate before a planned or expected end. Do not try to persuade them to stay or return against their wishes and do not create bad feelings at the end. Do consider exploring reasons if the opportunity presents itself; and consider the pros and cons of making contact by letter.

76   Reiterate the expectation that counselling will definitely end

You will have made it plain from the beginning that you have a contract for brief counselling. Where your contract is for time-limited work, there will be no doubt about the ending, because it will be reinforced throughout counselling. But where it is not 'date-stamped' (in other words, where you have referred, for example, to ending 'in the summer'), the client may seek to avoid the subject or to extend the time of ending. Discuss the subject clearly. Accept it is as the norm that a contract for brief counselling should terminate within weeks of the expected end, rather than months. There needs to be a very good reason for you to change this, but there may sometimes be such a reason (for example, an unforeseen accident or loss in the client's life near the end of counselling). Some clients do react strongly to endings, perhaps because of 'unfinished business' from their past; in these cases, allow enough time to work on this as an issue in itself.

Look closely at issues of transference and countertransference when you feel unable to face termination as planned. Where resistance to ending is clearly yours, you need either to work on it or to keep it from intruding. But sometimes you will be picking up the client's anxiety about ending. Resist the temptation to protract the counselling. It is sometimes a good idea to warn clients that 'As we approach the end of our work, you may well find that your symptoms return or get worse temporarily'. Because relapses or the fear of a relapse is common towards the end of counselling, clients may wonder if they really are able to continue to make progress on their own, and they may therefore exhibit all their old anxiety responses. Your job in this situation is to emphasise the progress they have made, to manage the ending in such a way that coping skills are reinforced and morbid expectations of inability to cope are minimised.

Your model of working may, of course, affect your approach to ending. You may perhaps interpret your client's resistance to ending as a recapitulation of former losses. This can be a fruitful line of enquiry, but remember that such experiences are not common to all clients. Also remember not to use such instances as reasons, in themselves, to extend counselling. The short-term psychodynamic counsellors (Flegenheimer 1982) do not, on the whole, succumb to lengthening the counselling process; rather, they anticipate and work with the impact of expected loss reactions. You may well need to anticipate such material and raise it earlier and more deliberately than you might in long-term work. You may also need to remind your client of her original goals and help her to review how closely she has come to achieving them. So, barring very exceptional cases, remind the client that the end is in sight and stick to it.

* Summary: Repeat the expectation that counselling will definitely end and work explicitly towards this, avoiding any temptation to lengthen the contract, except in rare circumstances.

---

77   Encourage final feedback

It is a good practice to address the subject of ending explicitly and to include in that discussion a review of the whole counselling experience. Accept that for some clients termination is *not* critical and painful; but still convey the idea that it is useful to look back at what has been learned in counselling and what can be taken further in the client's life. Make it easy for clients to collect their thoughts about counselling and express their feelings towards you. You may find it useful to do this systematically, but you obviously need to be sensitive to individual clients' feelings on ending counselling. So with some clients you may run through a checklist of what they consider has been helpful and unhelpful, and with others you may talk more generally.

Garfield (1989: 98) gives an example of how the client's disappointment with the rate of progress can be discussed in the middle phase of counselling. Obviously such disappointment is likely to surface before the very end, except perhaps in the case of very compliant and unassertive clients. But you may be faced with certain areas of disappointment at the end. Sometimes a client may say, 'Well, I do feel a lot better on the whole, even though things are still not what I'd hoped'. In such a case, try to elicit the nature of this disappointment. Help the client to spell out exactly how things are better and how they are not. It may turn out that you have failed to address certain areas of the client's concerns (in your enthusiasm for looking at other areas).

But it is likely that your client is either minimising the gains he has made, or is, perhaps, lamenting the fact that life itself is still not problem-free. Tease out the elements of statements of disappointment, acknowledging any genuine dissatisfaction with counselling, but also encouraging the client to take responsibility for himself and for any unrealistic demands that life should meet his needs. To borrow from transactional analysis, when he speaks from his 'Child' at the end of counselling, remind him to maintain an Adult perspective on this. Capitalise on what has been learned in counselling to show your client that he can still make a lot of progress himself after counselling.

Allow and reciprocate both disappointment and gratitude. If your client's temperament is such that he feels very emotional on ending and wishes to be demonstrative, do not discourage this. Depending on your own counselling orientation and your personality, you may be more or less happy to join with your client in emotional feedback. Broadly speaking, the more humanistic practitioners engage freely in spontaneous emotional displays, while psychodynamic and cognitive-behavioural practitioners may be rather more reserved. Our advice is that you respond in a way that is congruent with your own style, your client's style, and the relationship you have built up between you. Avoid a falsely 'professional' or a falsely 'intimate' ending. Genuinely respond, likewise, to any gifts that the client may offer you. While some counsellors do refuse gifts on principle, we believe it is more appropriate to allow clients to give freely if they wish to do so.

Consider what you will do in the event that a client discloses totally new material at this stage. For example, in reviewing the course of counselling, the client may say, 'Well, it occurs to me that I've never said much about my sex life' or 'I think I mentioned it once, but I haven't gone much into the time in my life when I was abused'. This may present a real temptation to extend counselling. But you may have picked up earlier your client's tendency to issue 'last minute' statements. If such a disclosure is made, then suggest to the client that this is something it may be important to reflect on and to consider whether she wishes explicitly to work on it at a later time with you, or with another practitioner. Budman and Gurman (1988) emphasise the importance of adhering to present goals and if necessary seeing clients at a later time to address further issues. Don't be afraid that the client will fall apart or that you are failing in your responsibilities as a counsellor by not addressing every issue. There is ample evidence (see, for example, Kupers 1988) that clients often make their way from one counsellor to another, over the course of years, as they feel appropriate. We believe, with Budman and Gurman, that clients may also quite legitimately return for counselling with the same counsellor at different times. A note of caution, here, however. When clients nervously ask you if they can return, should they run into difficulties, consider the wisdom of reminding them of how much they have learned, of the extent of their own resources and their ability to cope. Suggest to them that they try out what skills and strategies they have learned, before automatically resorting to further counselling.

* Summary: Deliberately encourage discussion of ending and of the counselling process as a whole, including issues of disappointment, gratitude and remaining fears. Remind clients of what they have learned and reinforce their coping skills.

---

78 Consider the advantages and disadvantages of different kinds of endings

---

There is no one right way to terminate counselling, as we have said. It will be apparent from the rest of this book that there are different approaches to brief counselling and its management. We have mentioned time-limited and brief counselling models. There is also the question of fixed or staggered or tapered endings; of serial counselling (repeated courses of counselling over a span, perhaps, of years); and of follow-ups. At some stage in your work, you will find it necessary to consider the merits and demerits of each of these methods of ending.

Sledge et al. (1990) discussed the differences between time-limited counselling, where an ending date is fixed in advance and the number of sessions is not negotiable: brief counselling, where there is an understanding that counselling will last a few months, but no specific ending date is set in advance; and open-ended counselling, which involves no disussion of an ending date. Sledge et al.'s study suggests that a strictly time-limited contract reduces the likelihood of people dropping out of counselling. It may, therefore, be particularly containing for some clients who exhibit anxiety about an indefinite period in counselling. Mann

(1973) capitalises on the advantages of a fixed time limit. It gives clients a rather dramatic focus and is likely to shake up ambivalence: clients know they will not get the chance for 'last minute confessions' and delays. But, equally, time-limited work may not be effective for certain clients – perhaps those who feel heavily pressurised by time constraints in their everyday life. Time-limited work also requires a certain quality of concentration and commitment from practitioners, which may or may not suit your style. Note, too, that cognitive-analytic therapy (Ryle 1990) demands a considerable amount of homework from both client and counsellor, in addition to work within the time-limited contract. Time-limited work allows clients to calculate exactly how much it will cost them financially: it also allows counselling agencies to plan services more effectively.

Brief counselling which has no set ending date is likely to help clients feel relaxed and able to explore without pressure. You need to convey, in your initial discussions, some idea of how long this kind of contract may run to. You may state this in terms of 'a few months', 'about six months' or 'less than a year', but however it is explained it is a good idea to reflect on the possibility of any misunderstandings between you and your client. As we have said earlier, most counselling and therapy is in reality brief, lasting a few weeks or months. It can be useful to focus on this, therefore, and to introduce it into conversation with your clients. How do they feel about time constraints? Relieved or anxious? Indifferent? Obviously individual clients react differently. Some clients, told that you would like to see them for a few weeks, may be alarmed at how long counselling will take and that it may imply that they are a 'serious case'. To other clients, a few weeks seems like no time at all. These matters should have been discussed early in the counselling process, but they may arise later. You may well wonder, half way through a counselling contract, what the best way to terminate it will be.

A time-limited ending presents no dilemma as to how to end. A disadvantage is that it may cut clients off with no opportunity to experiment with what they have learned. While some time-limited endings may stagger the last few sessions to allow clients to integrate what they have learned, some do not. Date-unspecified brief counselling allows you the flexibility to stagger or taper the final sessions. You might, for example, suggest to your client that she moves from weekly to fortnightly sessions, and then to monthly, in order to test for herself how able she is independently to put into practice her new skills. Exactly what kind of ending you propose to each client will depend on client differences that you have become aware of: on the nature and severity of your clients' problems; and on clients' temperaments and learning styles. It is a good practice to combine particular homework assignments with such endings in order to test out gains and consolidate what has been achieved.

Budman and Gurman (1988) are in favour of staggered endings which allow clients to move their focus from counselling to real life. Their model also places emphasis on counselling as a serial process; clients may return at a later date with another issue. Counselling is regarded as a small part of life, appropriate for particular interpersonal, developmental and existential crises. If you are working in this way, perhaps in a clinic setting, or in private practice, we would encourage you to consider its benefits and ethos. This way of working is appropriate to many people, it is cost-effective to clients and some service-providers, but may be more difficult for you as the counsellor to manage. Many counsellors in fact practise sporadic counselling, seeing a client for a few months, for example, then having a gap, then resuming work for a further period. This is sometimes orientated to different client issues, and sometimes to clients' finances.

You also need to consider the value of follow-up sessions. Some practitioners make a habit of suggesting a single follow-up session three, four or six months after termination. This is in order to check on how firmly clients have consolidated their gains in counselling. It also gives them the opportunity to reflect back on what they have learned. In addition it is experienced by many people as containing – knowing that the counsellor retains an interest in them and is available in the future. It also gives you an opportunity to review your work and to learn with hindsight what the client found most helpful or unhelpful. One function of such a session can be to act as a booster, reinforcing previous gains in counselling. Consider the value of offering such 'top-up' sessions either on a one-off basis or from time to time.

We trust that this variety of endings conveys our belief that there is not a right way to end. There is sometimes a certain mystique in some models of counselling, or in some training institutes, about correct and immutable ways of beginning and ending. Our preference is to remain sensitised to the needs of each client and to make judgements regarding such arrangements that will best suit clients' temperaments, learning styles, expectations and wallets! We realise that there are pressures on counsellors in certain settings (not least in private practice) either to terminate promptly with clients or to keep clients for a long period of time. We would urge practitioners and service managers and funders to consider the value of flexibility to meet clients' real needs. Invite your clients' opinions on the best kinds of endings for them when it is apparent that they have some understanding of how counselling works, and when they have achieved at least some of their goals.

* Summary: Examine the advantages and disadvantages of various ways of ending your work with clients, and base your decisions on clients' needs. Balance your own preferences against the possible advantages of date-specific and staggered endings; consider serial counselling, and follow-up sessions.

---

79   Let the client know that ending counselling sometimes (but not inevitably) engenders feelings of loss

---

Psychodynamic counsellors in particular may be inclined to anticipate loss reactions in their clients as the end is approached. (They will also look for significant client reactions to holidays and breaks.) Our position is that experiences of loss and separation vary considerably from client to client. This is the position, too, of Garfield (1989), who suggests that for most clients in brief counselling endings are natural, non-traumatic events. Given the brevity of brief counselling, it is likely that very intimate bonds will not occur frequently: or that those strong bonds which do occur will be modified by an emphasis on goalsetting and problem-solving. Do not add to clients' problems by encouraging them to become dependent on you. We do not advocate aloofness, but we concur here with Mahrer (1989) who places the emphasis in counselling on the clients being in touch with their own inner world and making changes in their real life, and not on forming a special relationship with the counsellor. If you follow Budman and Gurman's (1988: 11) view that 'being in the world is more important than being in therapy', you will convey this attitude to clients throughout the counselling process. If you are committed to a long-term, transference-based model of counselling or therapy, you are likely to emphasise the nature of the relationship with you and quite possibly de-emphasise clients' progress in their everyday life.

In spite of what we have said here, some clients will experience the end of counselling as difficult. It may restimulate old experiences of painful partings. Or it may be that clients are unconvinced that they will be able to cope without you. Clients' progress is sometimes deceptive; people may do very well in counselling while they have you to confer with, but feel bereft and unprepared at the prospect of losing you. In this case, your task is to remind clients how much they have achieved, how much they have learned to generalise to different situations, and how important it is to test out those gains in real life. If you have emphasised homework, for example, you have prepared the ground for your clients to work on their own concerns confidently. If you have not used homework or other means of encouraging the client to work towards independence outside of the counselling session, find a way of helping the client to work on her own concerns.

One means of encouraging the expression of feelings on ending is written work which reviews what has happened in counselling. The cognitive-analytic practice of the client and counsellor writing 'goodbye letters' to each other is an excellent example of this (Appendix 7). It is a channel for clients to order their feelings and to put them into perspective. You may devise your own ways of dealing with strong feelings on ending. If you work humanistically, strong feelings may feature prominently in your work and may help the client to regard strong feelings as normal and acceptable, and not as threats to their integrity or ability to cope. Some counsellors (e.g. Mearns and Thorne 1988) may readily display their own feelings of loss and sadness on ending, thus communicating to clients that it is perfectly acceptable to experience and show those feelings, and that one can survive them! The key here is, of course, to be flexible towards your clients' needs, while being true to your own way of working.

* **Summary: Do not expect all clients to go through the same reactions to ending counselling. Encourage clients to use what comes up at the end for further learning opportunities. Accept whatever genuine, strong feelings are displayed by clients at the end.**

---

80 Help clients to use what they have learned to look positively towards the future

---

Budman and Gurman (1988: 11) state their belief that the brief therapist 'accepts that many changes will occur "after therapy" and will not be observable to the therapist'. They are content to help clients on their way, rather than nurse them through a mythical, once-and-for-all therapy process. Similarly, if you practise a form of counselling that is brief and which has faith in the 'adult developmental perspective' of learning, then you will probably often be in a position where you are not witness to dramatic and gratifying changes in your clients. It is obviously easier to convey a faith in your clients' ability to continue to put their learning gains into operation 'after counselling' if you yourself believe in such a process.

Melges (1982) actually makes the sense of the future central in his model of future-oriented psychotherapy, arguing that clients' temporal distortions play a large part in their psychopathology. He uses a form of brief eclectic therapy which strives to correct distorted views of the future. You may not have such an orientation, but all counselling models implicitly aim at changing an unsatisfactory past or present into a more satisfying present or future. Models like transactional analysis work on the premise that lifelong scripts can be changed by present 'redecisions' and by achieving full contact with the here and now.

All models of counselling should have an in-built mechanism for making clients their own counsellors. Some models do this explicitly. Rational-emotive therapy, which relies heavily on teaching clients to monitor and challenge their irrational thinking, places a lot of weight on homework assignments, for example. Perhaps person-centred counselling aims at the same ends in its own way. Gendlin (1984: 76), for example, discusses the concept of 'the client's client'. Gendlin explains how a client learns to focus on his 'felt sense' so that he achieves mastery of 'process steps' in counselling which constitute a 'carrying forward' of new experience. The client becomes his own client and his own counsellor. We have discussed earlier how it is sometimes useful for some clients to utilise an image of the counsellor temporarily. At the ending phase this may be appropriate for some clients, but it is obviously more desirable that most clients should have truly internalised the means to coping or living more fully.

Reinforce your client's hopes and expectations for further change by referring to the nature of learning: people do not stop learning as soon as they leave a particular situation. Many people learn more after they leave school, for example, than they learned while there. People learn formally how to drive while having driving instruction, but the real learning – coping with driving alone and unprotected by 'L' plates – is done after passing the test. It may be helpful to use such analogies with doubtful clients. Recalling our earlier references to client differences, you may also find it useful to make a point like this with clients who are, for example, 'medical modellers' (Richert 1983) by referring to appropriate literature from educational or counselling psychology which confirms that learning continues beyond the formal learning situation. You need to gauge your statements about the future to the client's situation in life; it may not be appropriate to insist with a client who is very old, for example, that they have a great deal to look forward to. In such a case, rethink and rephrase your intention: 'You have come a long way' or 'It looks as if you've found some of that peace you've been looking for' may be more fitting.

* Summary: Help your clients to look forward by reminding them of what they have achieved; how they have dealt with obstacles and what they have gained mastery of. Sensitively encourage clients to reconsider their view of time.

---

81 Evaluate your clients' progress at the end of counselling and learn what you can from working with them

If you have practised using the reflection process throughout counselling, regularly asking for feedback from the client, then you have in fact been evaluating your work and your client's progress. Questions directed at how well your approach is working for the client, and how helpful your relationship is, for example, constitute elements of process research. Unfortunately this is not in any way foolproof, because your client may not like to offend you, may be unaware of certain negative factors, and so on. But it is a good indication of how counselling is progressing.

We have also suggested that you might use a simple progress chart (Appendix 6). These methods will give you and your client a fair idea of how counselling is going.

It can be very useful for you to evaluate an entire counselling process after it has ended. Garfield (1989) recommends that you carry out a specific evaluation of your work, for example by using or devising appropriate forms (Appendix 8). The value of such evaluation lies in what can be learned from unique cases and in getting into the habit of objective self-assessment. Garfield suggests in particular that counsellors attend to the presenting complaint in their post-counselling evaluations, because there is a temptation to address everything *but* this. You may dislike the idea of formally evaluating your work, but we consider that if you devise your own means of doing such research, you are likely to learn a lot from it. Questions you might like to ask yourself include: did the client attain or closely approach his goals? Did the client change measurably? Was the client satisfied? How is the client's achievement to be explained? What could have been more helpful? Were there particular errors I made as a counsellor? What have I learned from working with this person?

We have said that it is better to accept that you will sometimes make mistakes, rather than compounding the problem by berating yourself for making them. We don't suggest that you become blasé about errors, but that you keep them in proportion. We also commend the practice of ironing out errors by using the reflection process. Show your clients that you can get things wrong, or that you are open to correction; let them know that you have their interests at heart more than any preoccupation with professional perfectionism. Sachs (1983) concluded a study of negative outcomes in brief therapy by finding that counsellor errors clearly predicted such outcomes. Davis (1989) drew the conclusion from this that you would do well to attend to minimising errors rather than striving for perfection. You can minimise errors by closely monitoring your counselling (for example, by tape-recording); by regularly taking your work to supervision; and by regularly inviting feedback from clients. Do this in a spirit of open learning, rather than of defensive anxiety, and you are very likely to reduce errors considerably. Also, we hope that by using a text such as this you will become aware of what works well for your style of counselling, what you may be avoiding, and what you can most usefully take to supervision. You may well disagree with some of what you read here, and if such disagreement at least provokes thought and further evaluation, then we believe we have achieved our purpose in writing this book.

* Summary: Find a method of evaluating your counselling which gets you into the habit of assessing your work and helps you to reduce errors. Learn what you can from working with each client and refer your reflections to supervision.

AFTERWORD

After you have completed your initial training and begun practising as a counsellor, new questions will become meaningful for you. We hope that the practical advice in this book will stimulate you to reflect on your work. We suggest that if you are interested in following up certain areas in slightly greater depth (for example, issues of therapeutic alliance) you might read *Key Issues for Counselling in Action* (Dryden 1989).

The combination of putting training into practice and taking practice issues to supervision is the key development for beginners. But as you progress, you will want to know what is happening in the field generally. We suggest you consult the following: the *British Journal of Guidance and Counselling*, the *Counseling Psychologist*, *Counselling Psychology Quarterly*, the *Journal of Counseling Psychology*, the *Journal of Counseling and Development*, and *Counselling: The Journal of the British Association for Counselling*.

The third edition of the *Handbook of Psychotherapy and Behavior Change* (Garfield and Bergin 1986) is a key source of research information on many aspects of therapy and counselling, and you are advised at least to have a look at the variety of topics covered there and their implications for practice. (Look out for future editions of the *Handbook*.) Remember when you do so, however, always to balance such findings against the individual needs and realities of each of your clients.

You may also find the *Diagnostic and Statistical Manual* (third edition, revised, 1987) a useful source of information on the classification of psychological disturbances. While many counsellors dislike the very idea of classification, and there is certainly a case for being critical of many of the classifications in the DSM III R, it is instructive to become aware of psychiatric terminology. You might also look at the *International Classification of Diseases* (ninth edition), which is an alternative source of classification produced by the World Health Organisation. (The fourth edition of the *DSM* and the tenth edition of the *ICD* are both imminent at the time of writing.)

Where your interest is in establishing local professional contacts or looking for counsellors to whom you might refer clients, consult the *Counselling and Psychotherapy Resources Directory* of the British Association for Counselling.

APPENDIX 1
Stages of change questionnaire

Stages of change scale

Name: _____

Each statement describes how a person might feel about his or her problems. Please indicate the extent to which you tend to agree or disagree with each statement. In each case, make your choice in terms of how you feel **right now**, not what you have felt in the past or would like to feel.

There are **FIVE** possible responses to each of the questionnaire items:

1 = Strongly Disagree (SD)
2 = Disagree (D)
3 = Undecided (U)
4 = Agree (A)
5 = Strongly Agree (SA)

Circle the number that best describes how much you agree or disagree with each statement.

		SD	D	U	A	SA
1	As far as I'm concerned, I don't have any problems that need changing.	1	2	3	4	5
2	I think I might be ready for some self-improvement.	1	2	3	4	5
3	I am doing something about the problems that had been bothering me.	1	2	3	4	5
4	It might be worthwhile to work on my problems.	1	2	3	4	5
5	I'm not the problem one. It doesn't make much sense for me to be here.	1	2	3	4	5

Name:_____

		SD	D	U	A	SA
6	It worries me that I might slip back on problems I have already changed, so I am ready to work on my problems.	1	2	3	4	5
7	I am finally doing some work on my problems.	1	2	3	4	5
8	I've been thinking that I might want to change something about myself.	1	2	3	4	5
9	I have been successful in working on my problems but I'm not sure I can keep up the effort on my own.	1	2	3	4	5
10	At times my problems are difficult, but I'm working on them.	1	2	3	4	5
11	Working on problems is pretty much of a waste of time for me because the problems don't have to do with me.	1	2	3	4	5
12	I'm working on my problems in order to better understand myself.	1	2	3	4	5
13	I guess I have faults, but there's nothing that I really need to change.	1	2	3	4	5
14	I am really working hard to change.	1	2	3	4	5
15	I have problems and I really think I should work on them.	1	2	3	4	5
16	I'm not following through with what I had already changed as well as I had hoped, and I'm working to prevent a relapse of my problems.	1	2	3	4	5
17	Even though I'm not always successful in changing, I am at least working on my problems.	1	2	3	4	5
18	I thought once I had resolved my problems I would be free of them, but sometimes I still find myself struggling with them.	1	2	3	4	5
19	I wish I had more ideas on how to solve my problems.	1	2	3	4	5
20	I have started working on my problems but I would like help.	1	2	3	4	5
21	Maybe someone will be able to help me.	1	2	3	4	5
22	I may need a boost right now to help me maintain the changes I've already made.	1	2	3	4	5
23	I may be part of the problem, but I don't really think I am.	1	2	3	4	5

Name:_____

		SD	D	U	A	SA
24	I hope that someone will have some good advice for me.	1	2	3	4	5
25	Anyone can talk about changing; I'm actually doing something about it.	1	2	3	4	5
26	All this talk about psychology is boring. Why can't people just forget about their problems?	1	2	3	4	5
27	I'm working to prevent myself from having a relapse of my problems.	1	2	3	4	5
28	It is frustrating, but I feel I might be having a recurrence of a problem I thought I had resolved.	1	2	3	4	5
29	I have worries but so does the next person. Why spend time thinking about them?	1	2	3	4	5
30	I am actively working on my problems.	1	2	3	4	5
31	I would rather cope with my faults than try to change them.	1	2	3	4	5
32	After all I had done to try and change my problems, every now and again they come back to haunt me.	1	2	3	4	5

Scoring of the stages of change scale

- The following are Pre-Contemplation items:
  1, 5, 11, 13, 23, 26, 29, 31
- The following are Contemplation items:
  2, 4, 8, 12, 15, 19, 21, 24
- The following are Action items:
  3, 7, 10, 14, 17, 20, 25, 30
- The following are Maintenance items:
  6, 9, 16, 18, 22, 27, 28, 32

The scale is designed to be a continuous measure. Thus, subjects can score high on more than one of the four stages.

Because the scale is still being validated, it is available only for research purposes. Therefore, to date there have been no cut-off norms established to determine what constitutes high, medium or low on a particular stage. And, again, the stages are considered to be continuous and not discreet.

APPENDIX 2
Opinions about psychological problems questionnaire: Causes of psychological problems

Opinions about psychological problems

This questionnaire has two parts. The first asks about how you view the *causes* of your problems; the second asks how you think these problems can be *helped*.

Causes of psychological problems

People have different views about what causes psychological problems. The following questions ask for your opinion of the causes of your *own* problems. There are no right or wrong answers: your own opinion is what counts. Please indicate how much you agree or disagree with each statement by using the following scale. Circle one number for each statement.

Disagree Strongly	Disagree Moderately	Disagree Mildly	Agree Mildly	Agree Moderately	Agree Strongly
−3	−2	−1	+1	+2	+3

My problems are caused by	Disagree Strongly	Disagree Moderately	Disagree Mildly	Agree Mildly	Agree Moderately	Agree Strongly
1 Feelings that are buried out of sight.	−3	−2	−1	+1	+2	+3

My problems are caused by	Disagree Strongly	Disagree Moderately	Disagree Mildly	Agree Mildly	Agree Moderately	Agree Strongly
2 Illogical beliefs.	-3	-2	-1	+1	+2	+3
3 Other people not accepting me for who I am.	-3	-2	-1	+1	+2	+3
4 Becoming too anxious in certain situations.	-3	-2	-1	+1	+2	+3
5 A disorder of the brain or nervous system.	-3	-2	-1	+1	+2	+3
6 Worrying too much about what other people think of me.	-3	-2	-1	+1	+2	+3
7 Exaggerating the importance of things that may happen.	-3	-2	-1	+1	+2	+3
8 Unemployment or an unsatisfactory job.	-3	-2	-1	+1	+2	+3
9 Events that happened in childhood.	-3	-2	-1	+1	+2	+3
10 Having learnt bad habits over the years.	-3	-2	-1	+1	+2	+3
11 An inherited physical cause.	-3	-2	-1	+1	+2	+3
12 Repeating old patterns in relationships with other people.	-3	-2	-1	+1	+2	+3
13 Hiding feelings from friends or family.	-3	-2	-1	+1	+2	+3
14 Lack of money.	-3	-2	-1	+1	+2	+3
15 Running away from responsibilities.	-3	-2	-1	+1	+2	+3
16 Repressing basic human impulses.	-3	-2	-1	+1	+2	+3
17 Thinking about myself too much.	-3	-2	-1	+1	+2	+3
18 Having learnt the wrong reactions to certain situations.	-3	-2	-1	+1	+2	+3
19 Unsatisfactory means of transport.	-3	-2	-1	+1	+2	+3
20 Not paying attention to my feelings.	-3	-2	-1	+1	+2	+3
21 Making harsh judgements of myself.	-3	-2	-1	+1	+2	+3
22 A lack of will power.	-3	-2	-1	+1	+2	+3

My problems are caused by	Disagree Strongly	Disagree Moderately	Disagree Mildly	Agree Mildly	Agree Moderately	Agree Strongly
23 Not accepting myself for who I am.	−3	−2	−1	+1	+2	+3
24 Conflicting feelings about my parents when I was young.	−3	−2	−1	+1	+2	+3
25 Dissatisfaction with the community I live in.	−3	−2	−1	+1	+2	+3
26 Not having a realistic view of the good and the bad things that have happened.	−3	−2	−1	+1	+2	+3
27 Conflicts in my unconscious mind.	−3	−2	−1	+1	+2	+3
28 Illness, such as colds or flu.	−3	−2	−1	+1	+2	+3
29 The state of the economy.	−3	−2	−1	+1	+2	+3
30 Unrealistic thinking.	−3	−2	−1	+1	+2	+3
31 Rewards or punishments received in the past.	−3	−2	−1	+1	+2	+3
32 A conscience that won't let me alone.	−3	−2	−1	+1	+2	+3
33 Not liking myself.	−3	−2	−1	+1	+2	+3
34 Having unrealistic expectations.	−3	−2	−1	+1	+2	+3
35 Something going wrong with my body.	−3	−2	−1	+1	+2	+3
36 Not understanding what I really feel inside.	−3	−2	−1	+1	+2	+3
37 Laziness.	−3	−2	−1	+1	+2	+3
38 Not having learnt the right ways to cope with certain situations.	−3	−2	−1	+1	+2	+3
39 Not being true to myself.	−3	−2	−1	+1	+2	+3
40 Other people being unreasonable.	−3	−2	−1	+1	+2	+3
41 Putting myself down for no reason.	−3	−2	−1	+1	+2	+3
42 Poor housing.	−3	−2	−1	+1	+2	+3
43 The wrong balance of chemicals in my body.	−3	−2	−1	+1	+2	+3
44 Bad luck or fate.	−3	−2	−1	+1	+2	+3
45 Having learnt wrong ways of doing things from someone else.	−3	−2	−1	+1	+2	+3

My problems are caused by	Disagree Strongly	Disagree Moderately	Disagree Mildly	Agree Mildly	Agree Moderately	Agree Strongly
46 Unsatisfactory relationships with other people.	−3	−2	−1	+1	+2	+3
47 It's impossible to explain the cause of my problems.	−3	−2	−1	+1	+2	+3

If you think there are other important causes not listed above, please add them here:

Opinions about psychological problems

Etiology   Item Key (3/83)

My problems are caused by

Psychodynamic
1 Feelings that are buried out of sight.
9 Events that happened in childhood.
12 Repeating old patterns in relationships with other people.
16 Repressing basic human impulses.
24 Conflicting feelings about my parents when I was young.
27 Conflicts in my unconscious mind.
32 A conscience that won't let me alone.

Humanistic/Interpersonal
3 Other people not accepting me for who I am.
13 Hiding feelings from friends or family.
20 Not paying attention to my feelings.
23 Not accepting myself for who I am.
33 Not liking myself.
36 Not understanding what I really feel inside.
39 Not being true to myself.
46 Unsatisfactory relationships with other people.

Behavioural

4   Becoming too anxious in certain situations.
10 Having learnt bad habits over the years.
18 Having learnt the wrong reactions to certain situations.
31 Rewards or punishments received in the past.
38 Not having learnt the right ways to cope with certain situations.
45 Having learnt wrong ways of doing things from someone else.

Cognitive

2   Illogical beliefs.
6   Worrying too much about what other people think of me.
7   Exaggerating the importance of things that may happen.
21 Making harsh judgements of myself.
26 Not having a realistic view of the good and the bad things that have happened.
30 Unrealistic thinking.
34 Having unrealistic expectations.
41 Putting myself down for no reason.

Organic

5   A disorder of the brain or nervous system.
11 An inherited physical cause.
28 Illness, such as colds or flu.
35 Something going wrong with my body.
43 The wrong balance of chemicals in my body.

Social/Economic

8   Unemployment or an unsatisfactory job.
14 Lack of money.
19 Unsatisfactory means of transport.
25 Dissatisfaction with the community I live in.
29 The state of the economy.
42 Poor housing.

Naive

15 Running away from responsibilities.
17 Thinking about myself too much.
22 A lack of will power.
37 Laziness.
40 Other people being unreasonable.
44 Bad luck or fate.
47 It's impossible to explain the cause of my problems.

APPENDIX 3
Opinions about psychological problems questionnaire: Help for psychological problems

Opinions about psychological problems

Help for psychological problems

People have different views about what may help psychological problems. The following questions ask for your opinion of how your *own* problems could be helped. There are no right or wrong answers: your own opinion is what counts. Please indicate how much you agree or disagree with each statement by using the following scale. Circle one number for each statement.

Disagree Strongly	Disagree Moderately	Disagree Mildly	Agree Mildly	Agree Moderately	Agree Strongly
−3	−2	−1	+1	+2	+3

A good way to help my problems would be	Disagree Strongly	Disagree Moderately	Disagree Mildly	Agree Mildly	Agree Moderately	Agree Strongly
1 Taking the attitude that I should count my blessings, rather than looking on the dark side of things.	−3	−2	−1	+1	+2	+3
2 Having an expert show me how to think in a more logical way.	−3	−2	−1	+1	+2	+3
3 Getting tablets to regulate my mood.	−3	−2	−1	+1	+2	+3

A good way to help my problems would be	Disagree Strongly	Disagree Moderately	Disagree Mildly	Agree Mildly	Agree Moderately	Agree Strongly
4 Learning to pay attention to my feelings.	-3	-2	-1	+1	+2	+3
5 Discussing the problems with someone in an honest, person-to-person way.	-3	-2	-1	+1	+2	+3
6 Understanding the childhood origins of the problems.	-3	-2	-1	+1	+2	+3
7 Having an expert teach me better ways of reacting to certain situations.	-3	-2	-1	+1	+2	+3
8 Getting medication.	-3	-2	-1	+1	+2	+3
9 Better housing.	-3	-2	-1	+1	+2	+3
10 Having an expert point out the meaning of my dreams and fantasies.	-3	-2	-1	+1	+2	+3
11 An improvement in the economy.	-3	-2	-1	+1	+2	+3
12 Examining, with an expert, what situations make the problems better or worse.	-3	-2	-1	+1	+2	+3
13 Talking to an expert about my relationship with my parents when I was young.	-3	-2	-1	+1	+2	+3
14 Having someone listen to my feelings without giving advice.	-3	-2	-1	+1	+2	+3
15 Worrying less about what other people think of me.	-3	-2	-1	+1	+2	+3
16 Learning to live with the problems, rather than trying to change them.	-3	-2	-1	+1	+2	+3
17 Being shown by an expert how to change my outlook on the problems.	-3	-2	-1	+1	+2	+3
18 Learning to accept myself for who I am.	-3	-2	-1	+1	+2	+3
19 Taking my mind off myself.	-3	-2	-1	+1	+2	+3
20 Having medical treatment to put the chemicals of my body back into balance.	-3	-2	-1	+1	+2	+3
21 A better community to live in.	-3	-2	-1	+1	+2	+3

A good way to help my problems would be	Disagree Strongly	Disagree Moderately	Disagree Mildly	Agree Mildly	Agree Moderately	Agree Strongly
22 Learning the skills needed in difficult situations.	−3	−2	−1	+1	+2	+3
23 Putting my bad feelings aside, so I can feel more cheerful.	−3	−2	−1	+1	+2	+3
24 Tackling the problems in a planned, step-by-step way.	−3	−2	−1	+1	+2	+3
25 Learning to think more realistically.	−3	−2	−1	+1	+2	+3
26 Having other people change, rather than changing myself.	−3	−2	−1	+1	+2	+3
27 Having an expert teach me specific ways to change my behaviour.	−3	−2	−1	+1	+2	+3
28 Discovering what I really feel inside.	−3	−2	−1	+1	+2	+3
29 Deciding to 'keep a stiff upper lip'.	−3	−2	−1	+1	+2	+3
30 Talking about my feelings to someone I trust.	−3	−2	−1	+1	+2	+3
31 Learning to think differently about the problems.	−3	−2	−1	+1	+2	+3
32 Having an expert analyse my unconscious reasons for doing things.	−3	−2	−1	+1	+2	+3
33 Keeping busy, so as not to think about the problems.	−3	−2	−1	+1	+2	+3
34 Hearing from other people that I am doing well or trying hard.	−3	−2	−1	+1	+2	+3
35 Getting a satisfactory job.	−3	−2	−1	+1	+2	+3
36 Learning to judge myself less harshly.	−3	−2	−1	+1	+2	+3
37 Talking to someone who listens closely to what I'm really saying.	−3	−2	−1	+1	+2	+3
38 Realizing how I repeat old patterns in relationships with other people.	−3	−2	−1	+1	+2	+3
39 Deciding to 'grin and bear it'.	−3	−2	−1	+1	+2	+3
40 Getting tablets.	−3	−2	−1	+1	+2	+3

A good way to help my problems would be	Disagree Strongly	Disagree Moderately	Disagree Mildly	Agree Mildly	Agree Moderately	Agree Strongly
41 Getting physically fit and healthy.	−3	−2	−1	+1	+2	+3
42 Having an expert point out that how I think about myself can sometimes be wrong.	−3	−2	−1	+1	+2	+3
43 Better means of transport.	−3	−2	−1	+1	+2	+3
44 Coming to understand feelings or impulses that I'm not aware of.	−3	−2	−1	+1	+2	+3
45 Having more money.	−3	−2	−1	+1	+2	+3
46 Using will power to overcome the problems.	−3	−2	−1	+1	+2	+3
47 There's nothing that can be done to help my problems.	−3	−2	−1	+1	+2	+3

If you think there are other ways in which your problems could be helped, please add them here:

Opinions about psychological problems

Treatment

A good way to help my problems would be

Psychodynamic
6 Understanding the childhood origins of the problems.
10 Having an expert point out the meaning of my dreams and fantasies.
13 Talking to an expert about my relationship with my parents when I was young.
32 Having an expert analyse my unconscious reasons for doing things.
38 Realizing how I repeat old patterns in relationships with other people.
44 Coming to understand feelings or impulses that I'm not aware of.

Humanistic/Interpersonal
 4 Learning to pay attention to my feelings.
 5 Discussing the problems with someone in an honest, person-to-person way.
14 Having someone listen to my feelings without giving advice.
18 Learning to accept myself for who I am.
28 Discovering what I really feel inside.
30 Talking about my feelings to someone I trust.
37 Talking to someone who listens closely to what I'm really saying.

Behavioural
 7 Having an expert teach me better ways of reacting to certain situations.
12 Examining, with an expert, what situations make the problems better or worse.
22 Learning the skills needed in difficult situations.
24 Tackling the problems in a planned, step-by-step way.
27 Having an expert teach me specific ways to change my behaviour.
34 Hearing from other people that I am doing well or trying hard.

Cognitive
 2 Having an expert show me how to think in a more logical way.
15 Worrying less about what other people think of me.
17 Being shown by an expert how to change my outlook on the problems.
25 Learning to think more realistically.
31 Learning to think differently about the problems.
36 Learning to judge myself less harshly.
42 Having an expert point out that how I think about myself can sometimes be wrong.

Organic
 3 Getting tablets to regulate my mood.
 8 Getting medication.
20 Having medical treatment to put the chemicals of my body back into balance.
40 Getting tablets.
41 Getting physically fit and healthy.

Social/Economic
 9 Better housing.
11 An improvement in the economy.
21 A better community to live in.
35 Getting a satisfactory job.
43 Better means of transport.
45 Having more money.

Naive

  1 Taking the attitude that I should count my blessings, rather than looking on the dark side of things.

16 Learning to live with the problems, rather than trying to change them.

19 Taking my mind off myself.

23 Putting my bad feelings aside, so I can feel more cheerful.

26 Having other people change, rather than changing myself.

29 Deciding to 'keep a stiff upper lip'.

33 Keeping busy, so as not to think about the problems.

39 Deciding to 'grin and bear it'.

46 Using will power to overcome the problems.

47 There's nothing that can be done to help my problems.

Opinions about psychological problems

Background information

Name:_____

2 Age: _____

3 Sex: M F

4 Location (where are you filling out this questionnaire?): _____

_____

5 What psychological problems were you thinking about while you were answering this questionnaire? _____

_____

_____

6 What problems are you currently seeking help for (if different from question 5 above)? _____

_____

_____

Thank you for completing this questionnaire.

APPENDIX 4
Possible reasons for not completing homework assignments questionnaire

Questionnaire for client to complete

The following is a list of reasons that various clients have given for not doing their self-help assignments during the course of therapy. Because the speed of improvement depends primarily on the amount of self-help assignments that you are willing to do, it is of great importance to pinpoint any reasons that you may have for not doing this work. It is important to look for these reasons at the time that you feel a reluctance to do your assignment or a desire to put off doing it. Hence, it is best to fill out this questionnaire at that time. If you have any difficulty filling out this form and returning it to the therapist, it might be best to do it together during a therapy session. (Rate each statement by ringing 'T' (True) or 'F' (False). 'T' indicates that you agree with it; 'F' means the statement does not apply at this time.)

1 It seems that nothing can help me so there is no point in trying. T / F
2 It wasn't clear, I didn't understand what I had to do. T / F
3 I thought that the particular method the therapist had suggested would not be helpful. I didn't really see the value of it. T / F
4 It seemed too hard. T / F
5 I am willing to do self-help assignments, but I keep forgetting. T / F
6 I did not have enough time. I was too busy. T / F
7 If I do something the therapist suggests I do it's not as good as if I come up with my own ideas. T / F
8 I don't really believe I can do anything to help myself. T / F
9 I have the impression the therapist is trying to boss me around or control me. T / F

10 I worry about the therapist's disapproval. I believe
   that what I do just won't be good enough for him/her. T / F
11 I felt too bad, sad, nervous, upset (underline the
   appropriate word(s)) to do it. T / F
12 It would have upset me to do the homework. T / F
13 It was too much to do. T / F
14 It's too much like going back to school again. T / F
15 It seemed to be mainly for the therapist's benefit. T / F
16 Self-help assignments have no place in therapy. T / F
17 Because of the progress I've made these assignments
   are likely to be of no further benefit to me. T / F
18 Because these assignments have not been helpful in
   the past, I couldn't see the point of doing this one. T / F
19 I don't agree with this particular approach to therapy. T / F
20 OTHER REASONS (Please write them.)

APPENDIX 5
Advantages and disadvantages of present and desired behaviour inventory

Advantages/benefits of present behaviour

Short-term advantages/benefits

For yourself
1 _____
2 _____
3 _____
4 _____
5 _____
6 _____
7 _____
8 _____
9 _____
10 _____

For the other person
1 _____
2 _____
3 _____
4 _____
5 _____
6 _____
7 _____
8 _____
9 _____
10 _____

Long-term advantages/benefits

For yourself
1 _____
2 _____
3 _____
4 _____
5 _____
6 _____
7 _____
8 _____
9 _____
10 _____

For the other person
1 _____
2 _____
3 _____
4 _____
5 _____
6 _____
7 _____
8 _____
9 _____
10 _____

Disadvantages/costs of present behaviour

Short-term disadvantages/costs

For yourself

1 _____
2 _____
3 _____
4 _____
5 _____
6 _____
7 _____
8 _____
9 _____
10 _____

For the other person

1 _____
2 _____
3 _____
4 _____
5 _____
6 _____
7 _____
8 _____
9 _____
10 _____

Long-term disadvantages/costs

For yourself

1 _____
2 _____
3 _____
4 _____
5 _____
6 _____
7 _____
8 _____
9 _____
10 _____

For the other person

1 _____
2 _____
3 _____
4 _____
5 _____
6 _____
7 _____
8 _____
9 _____
10 _____

Advantages/benefits of desired behaviour

Short-term advantages/benefits

For yourself

1 _____
2 _____
3 _____
4 _____
5 _____
6 _____
7 _____
8 _____
9 _____
10 _____

For the other person

1 _____
2 _____
3 _____
4 _____
5 _____
6 _____
7 _____
8 _____
9 _____
10 _____

Long-term advantages/benefits

For yourself
1 _____
2 _____
3 _____
4 _____
5 _____
6 _____
7 _____
8 _____
9 _____
10 _____

For the other person
1 _____
2 _____
3 _____
4 _____
5 _____
6 _____
7 _____
8 _____
9 _____
10 _____

Disadvantages/costs of desired behaviour

Short-term disadvantages/costs

For yourself
1 _____
2 _____
3 _____
4 _____
5 _____
6 _____
7 _____
8 _____
9 _____
10 _____

For the other person
1 _____
2 _____
3 _____
4 _____
5 _____
6 _____
7 _____
8 _____
9 _____
10 _____

Long-term disadvantages/costs

For yourself
1 _____
2 _____
3 _____
4 _____
5 _____
6 _____
7 _____
8 _____
9 _____
10 _____

For the other person
1 _____
2 _____
3 _____
4 _____
5 _____
6 _____
7 _____
8 _____
9 _____
10 _____

APPENDIX 6
Client progress chart

Instructions for completing progress chart

Having agreed which goal or goals you are working on with your counsellor, use this progress chart to record your own view of progress towards goals. Write on it a specific goal. Consider each week whether you
are moving towards or away from your goal (or not moving at all). Enter
what scores seem appropriate to you: + 5 means that you have attained
your goal (or that your original symptom or problem is gone); − 5 means
that matters (in relation to this specific goal) have got much worse.
Scores in between indicate degrees of improvement or deterioration, as
judged by you. Each week, mark your score on the chart with an x and
discuss it with your counsellor. Remember that you are not scoring
yourself but how much change there is in relation to your goal for change.

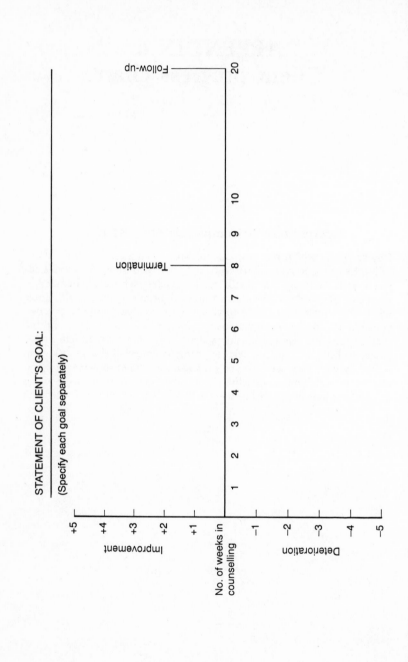

STATEMENT OF CLIENT'S GOAL:

(Specify each goal separately)

Improvement
+5
+4
+3
+2
+1

No. of weeks in counselling
1 2 3 4 5 6 7 8 9 10   20

Termination   Follow-up

Deterioration
−1
−2
−3
−4
−5

APPENDIX 7
Specimen 'goodbye letters'

Goodbye letter from a client in cognitive-analytic therapy to her therapist

Dear Barney,

These weeks of therapy have not been what I expected. I was worried that there would not be time enough to sort things out. I wanted the opportunity to talk exhaustively about all the things that had upset me in the past. It took a while for me to realise that this was not necessary and perhaps not even desirable. I found the middle sessions very difficult and felt quite discouraged about failure to get in touch with my hurt about my childhood. For me, the real revelation, the unexpected, was learning about self-sabotage. Before commencing therapy I wrote a list of some things I wanted to understand. The first point was why I was never properly prepared for examinations; it is really quite shocking to realise that one deliberately hurts oneself because fundamentally one feels unworthy. A related point was why I feel that I respect myself, and am confident in spite of evidence to the contrary. My major worry is that I will continue to spoil my chances. I feel that self-sabotage is deeply rooted and that it will take tremendous, sustained effort to combat it. I think it may be a long and uphill battle. The very positive thing that has emerged from therapy is the re-emergence of a 'lust for life'. There are so many things I want to enjoy, I have recovered a feeling of leaving therapy. Last week I felt ready for it, this week the fear that I may backslide is more prominent. If I'm honest I would like to have the continuous support of regular sessions until I feel more confident that I'm not going to undo the good work. Having said this, though, I do not feel I am about to be abandoned, the three-month follow-up session is a considerable solace. My relationship with my boyfriend still needs improving. As regards to the future, I want to continue to feel good about myself, to feel increasingly confident and to feel secure with this confidence, i.e. to know that it is a solid base and is not dependent upon props such as other people's opinions of me, or my career, etc. In brief, I want to be happy and autonomous and to feel that I have taken life in both hands. Perhaps I need some structured means of monitoring my progress by myself so that any backsliding can be arrested at the early stages.

Thank you, you've really helped me cut through the crap and to feel good and excited again.

Yours sincerely
Jasmine

Goodbye letter from a therapist to a client in cognitive-analytic therapy

Dear Ingrid,

Looking back at the time when you first came to therapy, you may recall your expectations of some miraculous cure for the frigidity both you and your husband put forth as being the major obstacle to your joint pursuit of happiness. Well, no miracles have taken place, yet now you feel like a sexually capable person – a far cry from feeling finished or burnt out and desperately seeking for miracles. More importantly, you have gained a sense of independence and of being very worthy to be respected by others. How were these changes brought about? The essential thing was that you gradually came to realise that frigidity was only the 'tip of the iceberg', the final expression of a whole constellation of pressures within the context of your important relationships. It both reflected the existence of a crucial problem in your life and a 'solution', however awkward or self-defeating the latter was. The problem consisted in establishing your independence while at the same time resentfully and placatingly committing yourself to your parents and to your husband without risking a choice. Frigidity, as a solution to this, enabled you to postpone making a choice without feeling responsible for this postponement. Now you don't need this any more; you have become your own agent, you have seen that you can be both tender and caring, and assert your own needs. What cut across the stalemate you were in, not daring to make any move, was the reinvestment in the positive aspects of yourself. You identified and worked upon the false dilemmas, the unobtrusive traps, the subtle snags which, you came to see, had dominated your way of dealing yourself and the others, and had kept you enmeshed in that wasteland of inertia, dissatisfaction, guilt and anger. Now you feel confident enough to renegotiate the terms of your relationship with your mother and with your husband. Perhaps this is what makes me, on my part, feel happy and optimistic about your future, whatever it may be.

Yours sincerely
Basil

APPENDIX 8
Case evaluation form

Case evaluation form

Case _____ Sex _____ Age _____ Referred by _____

Therapist _____ Supervisor _____

No. of interviews seen _____ No. of missed appointments _____

Referral or treatment problem(s) _____

_____

Possible changes at termination_____

_____

Recommendations for this case (if any)_____

_____

Rating scales

1 *Amount of change in client*
Please rate the *amount of change* you believe has occurred in this client
since he/she started therapy. Please do *not* rate on this scale the final
level of adjustment of the client. Rather, please rate the amount of *change*
or difference in functioning you believe has occurred in this client since
the beginning of therapy, regardless of how well or badly adjusted you
believe the client currently is and how much or how little work might
remain to be done in order for the client to be considered completely
healthy and well functioning.

_____ 1 Client has changed markedly for the worse.

_____ 2 Client has changed somewhat for the worse.

_____ 3 Client has changed slightly for the worse.

_____ 4 Client has shown essentially no change.

_____ 5 Client has changed slightly for the better.

_____ 6 Client has changed somewhat for the better.

_____ 7 Client has changed markedly for the better.

REFERENCES

Albee, G.W. (1990) The futility of psychotherapy *Journal of Mind and Behavior*, 11 (3 & 4), 369–84.

Amada, G. (1983) The interlude between short- and long-term psychotherapy *American Journal of Psychotherapy*, 37, 357–64.

Amato, R. and Bradshaw, R. (1985) An exploratory study of people's reasons for delaying or avoiding helpseeking *Australian Psychologist*, 20 (1), 21–31.

Balint, M., Ornstein, P.O. and Balint, E. (1972) *Focal Psychotherapy*. London: Tavistock.

Bellack, A.S. and Hersen, M. (1987) *Dictionary of Behavior Therapy Techniques*. Oxford: Pergamon.

Blackburn, I.-M. and Davidson, K. (1990) *Cognitive Therapy for Depression and Anxiety*. Oxford: Blackwell.

Bordin, E.S. (1979) The generalizability of the psychoanalytic concept of the working alliance *Psychotherapy: Theory, Research and Practice*, 16 (3), 252–60.

Brandt, L.W. (1982) *Psychologists Caught*. Toronto: University of Toronto Press.

Buber, M. (1947) *Between Man and Man*. London: Routledge & Kegan Paul.

Budman, S.H. (1990) The myth of termination in brief therapy. In J.K. Zeig and S.G. Gilligan (eds) *Brief Therapy: Myths, Methods and Metaphors*. New York: Brunner/Mazel.

Budman, S.H. and Gurman, A.S. (1988) *Theory and Practice of Brief Therapy*. London: Guilford.

Casement, P. (1985) *On Learning from the Patient*. London: Tavistock.

Clarkson, P. (1990) A multiplicity of psychotherapeutic relationships *British Journal of Psychotherapy*, 7 (2), 148–63.

Colson, D., Lewis, L. and Horwitz, L. (1985) Negative outcome in psychotherapy and psychoanalysis. In D.T. Mays and C.M. Franks (eds) *Negative Outcome in Psychotherapy and What To Do About It*. New York: Springer.

Davanloo, H. (1985) Short-term dynamic psychotherapy. In H. Kaplan and B.J. Sadock (eds) *Comprehensive Textbook of Psychiatry*. Baltimore, Md: Williams & Wilkins.

Davis, J. (1989) Issues in the evaluation of counsellors by supervisors *Counselling*, 69, 31–7.

Day, R.W. and Sparacio, R.T. (1989) Structuring the counselling process. In W. Dryden (ed.) *Key Issues for Counselling in Action*. London: Sage.

Dinnage, R. (1988) *One To One: Experiences of Psychotherapy*. London: Viking.

Dryden, W. (1982) *Social Problems: Treatment from a Rational-Emotive Perspective*. London: Institute for RET.

Dryden, W. (ed.) (1989) *Key Issues for Counselling in Action*. London: Sage.

Dryden, W. (1990) *Rational-Emotive Counselling in Action*. London: Sage.

Dryden, W. (1991) *Dryden on Counselling, Vol. 1: Seminal Papers*. London: Whurr.

Dryden, W. (1992) *The Dryden Interviews*. London: Whurr.

Durlak, J.A. (1979) Comparative effectiveness of paraprofessional and professional helpers *Psychological Bulletin*, 86 (1), 80–92.

Egan, G. (1990) *The Skilled Helper*, 4th edn. Pacific Grove, Calif.: Brooks/Cole.

Fairbairn, S. and Fairbairn G. (eds) (1987) *Psychology, Ethics and Change*. London: Routledge & Kegan Paul.

Flegenheimer, W.V. (1982) *Techniques of Brief Psychotherapy*. New York: Aronson.

Frances, A., Sweeney, J. and Clarkin, J. (1985) Do psychotherapies have specific effects? *American Journal of Psychotherapy*, 39 (2), 159–74.

Fransella, F. and Dalton, P. (1990) *Personal Construct Counselling in Action*. London: Sage.

Garfield, S.L. (1989) *The Practice of Brief Psychotherapy*. Oxford: Pergamon.

Garfield, S.L. and Bergin, A.E. (eds) (1986) *Handbook of Psychotherapy and Behavior Change*, 3rd edn. Chichester: Wiley.

Gendlin, E.T. (1984) The client's client: the edge of awareness. In R.F. Levant and J.M. Shlien (eds) *Client-Centered Therapy and the Person-Centered Approach*. New York: Praeger.

Glasser, W. (1984) *Take Effective Control of your Life*. New York: Harper & Row.

Heron, J. (1990) *Helping the Client*. London: Sage.

Hill, C. E. (1989) *Therapist Techniques and Client Outcomes*. London: Sage.

Hobson, R.E. (1985) *Forms of Feeling: The Heart of Psychotherapy*. London: Tavistock.

Holmes, J. and Lindley, R. (1989) *The Values of Psychotherapy*. Oxford: Oxford University Press.

Howard, G.S., Nance, D.W. and Myers, P. (1987) *Adaptive Counseling and Therapy*. San Francisco: Jossey Bass.

Ivey, A.E., Ivey, M.B. and Simek-Downing, L. (1987) *Counseling and Psychotherapy: Integrating Skills, Theory and Practice.* Englewood Cliffs, NJ: Prentice-Hall International.

Kopp, S.B. (1974) *If You Meet the Buddha on the Road, Kill Him!* London: Sheldon.

Koss, M.P. and Butcher, J.M. (1986) Research in brief psychotherapy. In S.L. Garfield and A.E. Bergin (3rd edn) (eds) *Handbook of Psychotherapy and Behavior Change.* Chichester: Wiley.

Kupers, T.A. (1988) *Ending Therapy.* London: New York University Press.

Lazarus, A.A. (1981) *The Practice of Multimodal Therapy.* New York: McGraw-Hill.

Lazarus, A.A. and Fay, A. (1990) Brief psychotherapy: tautology or oxymoron? In J.K. Zeig and S.G. Gilligan (eds) *Brief Therapy: Myths, Methods and Metaphors.* New York: Brunner/Mazel.

Levant, R.F. and Schlien, J.M. (eds) (1984) *Client-Centered Therapy and the Person-Centered Approach.* New York: Praeger.

Lewis, M.K., Rogers, C.R. and Shlien, J.M. (1959) Two cases of time-limited client-centered psychotherapy. In Burton, A. (ed.) *Case Studies of Counseling and Psychotherapy.* New York: Prentice-Hall.

Macaskill, N. (1985) Homework assignments in brief psychotherapy *British Journal of Psychotherapy,* 2 (2), 134–41.

Mahrer, A.R. (1988) The briefest psychotherapy *Changes,* 6 (3), 86–9.

Mahrer, A.R. (1989) *Experiential Psychotherapy: Basic Practices.* Ottawa, Canada: Ottawa University Press.

Malan, D.H. (1975) *A Study of Brief Psychotherapy.* London: Plenum.

Mann, J. (1973) *Time-limited Psychotherapy.* Cambridge, Mass.: Harvard University Press.

Marlatt, G.A. and Gordon, J. (eds) (1985) *Relapse Prevention.* New York: Guilford Press.

Mays, D.T. and Franks, C.M. (1985) *Negative Outcome in Psychotherapy and What to do about it.* New York: Springer.

Mearns, D. and Thorne, B. (1988) *Person-Centred Counselling in Action.* London: Sage.

Melges, F.T. (1982) *Time and the Inner Future: A Temporal Approach to Psychiatric Disorders.* New York: Wiley.

Nelson-Jones, R. (1989) *Effective Thinking Skills.* London: Cassell.

Omer, H. (1990) Enhancing the impact of therapeutic interventions *American Journal of Psychotherapy,* 44 (2), 218–31.

Orlinsky, D.E. and Howard, K.I. (1986) Process and outcome in psychotherapy. In S.L. Garfield and A.E. Bergin (3rd edn) (Eds) *Handbook of Psychotherapy and Behavior Change.* Chichester: Wiley.

Patten, M.I. and Walker, L.G. (1990) Marriage Guidance Counselling I: what clients think will help *British Journal of Guidance and Counselling,* 18 (1), 28–39.

Perry, S. (1989) Treatment time and the borderline patient: an under-appreciated strategy *Journal of Personality Disorders,* 3 (3), 230–9.

Pipes, R.B., Schwartz, R. and Crouch, P. (1985) Measuring client fears *Journal of Consulting and Clinical Psychology*, 53 (6), 933–4.

Prochaska, J.O. and DiClemente, C.C. (1984) *The Transtheoretical Approach*. Homewood, Ill.: Dow Jones-Irwin.

Rice, L.N. (1984) Client tasks in client-centered therapy. In R.F. Levant and J.M. Shlien (eds) *Client-Centered Therapy and the Person-Centered Approach*. New York: Praeger.

Richert, A. (1983) Differential prescription for psychotherapy on the basis of client role preferences *Psychotherapy: Theory, Research and Practice*, 20 (3), 321–9.

Rogers, C.R. (1990) *On Becoming a Person*. London: Constable.

Rosenbaum, R., Hoyt, M.F. and Talmon, M. (1990) The challenge of single-session therapies; creating pivotal moments. In R.A. Wells and V.J. Gianetti (eds) *Handbook of the Brief Psychotherapies*. New York: Plenum.

Rowan, J. (1988) The psychology of furniture *Counselling*, 64, 21–4.

Rowan, J. (1989) *The Reality Game*. London: Routledge.

Ryle, A. (1983) The value of written communications in dynamic psychotherapy *British Journal of Psychiatry*, 8, 195–8.

Ryle, A. (1990) *Cognitive-Analytic Therapy: Active Participation in Change*. Chichester: Wiley.

Sachs, J.S. (1983) Negative factors in brief psychotherapy: an empirical assessment *Journal of Consulting and Clinical Psychology*, 51, 557–64.

Scott, M. (1989) *A Cognitive-Behavioural Approach to Clients' Problems*. London: Routledge.

Sherman, R.T. and Anderson, C.A. (1987) Decreasing premature termination from psychotherapy *Journal of Social and Clinical Psychology*, 5 (3), 298–312.

Shlien, J.M., Mosak, H.H. and Dreikurs, R. (1962) Effect of time limits: a comparison of two psychotherapies *Journal of Consulting Psychology*, 9, 31–4.

Sifneos, P. (1972) *Short-Term Psychotherapy and Emotional Crisis*. Cambridge, Mass.: Harvard University Press.

Sklar, H. (1988) The impact of the therapeutic environment *Journal of Contemporary Psychotherapy*, 18 (2), 107–23.

Sledge, W.H., Moras, K., Hartley, D. and Levine, M.A. (1990) Effects of time-limited psychotherapy on patient drop-out rates *American Journal of Psychiatry*, 147 (10), 1342–7.

Stewart, I. (1989) *Transactional Analysis Counselling in Action*. London: Sage.

Stewart, I. and Joines, V. (1987) *T.A. Today*. Nottingham: Lifespace.

Storr, A. (1963) *The Integrity of the Personality*. Harmondsworth: Pelican.

Striano, J. (1988) *Can Psychotherapists Hurt You?* Santa Barbara, Calif: Professional Press.

Strupp, H.H. (1980) Success and failure in time-limited psychotherapy *Archives of General Psychiatry*, 37, 708–16.

Sutherland, S. (1989) *Breakdown*. London: Weidenfeld & Nicolson.

Sutton, C. (1989) The evaluation of counselling: a goal-attainment approach. In W. Dryden (ed.) *Key Issues for Counselling in Action*. London: Sage.

Toates, F (1990) *Obsessional Thoughts and Behaviour*. Wellingborough, Northants: Thorsons.

Ursano, R.J., Sonnenberg, S.M. and Lazar, S.G. (1991) *Psychodynamic Psychotherapy*. Washington, DC: American Psychiatric Press.

Van Deurzen-Smith, E. (1988) *Existential Counselling in Practice*. London: Sage.

Walker, L.G. and Patten, M.I. (1990) Marriage Guidance Counselling II: what counsellors want to give *British Journal of Guidance and Counselling*, 18 (3), 294–307.

Watkins, C.E. Jnr (1989) Countertransference: its impact on the counselling situation. In W. Dryden (ed.) *Key Issues for Counselling in Action*. London: Sage.

Wells, R.A. and Gianetti, V.J. (eds) (1990) *Handbook of the Brief Psychotherapies*. New York: Plenum.

Willer, B. and Miller, G.H. (1976) Client involvement in goal setting and its relationship to therapeutic outcome *Journal of Clinical Psychology*, 32 (3), 687–9.

Wolberg, L.R. (1980) *Handbook of Short-term Psychotherapy*. New York: Thieme-Stratton.

Yankura, J. and Dryden, W. (1990) *Doing RET: Albert Ellis in Action*. New York: Springer.

Zeig, J.K. (1990) Seeding. In J.K. Zeig and S.G. Gilligan (eds) *Brief Therapy: Myths, Methods and Metaphors*. New York: Brunner/Mazel.

INDEX